TEACHERS' NEEDS AND CONCERNS REGARDING READING INSTRUCTION

Findings, Strategies, and Applications

Edited by

Roger J. De Santi

University of New Orleans

UNIVERSITY
PRESS OF
AMERICA

LANHAM • NEW YORK • LONDON

Library of Congress Cataloging in Publication Data
Main entry under title:

Teachers' needs and concerns regarding reading instruction.

Includes index.
1. Reading (Elementary)–United States–Addresses,
essays, lectures. 2. Reading, Teachers of–United States –
Attitudes–Addresses, essays, lectures. I. De Santi, Roger
J.
LB1573.T35   1983   372.4   83–10219
ISBN 0–8191–3365–5
ISBN 0–8191–3366–3 (pbk.)

372.4
D441

ACKNOWLEDGEMENT

This material was partially supported and produced pursuant to a grant from the Department of Education, State of Louisiana, Bureau of Elementary Education, College Projects, Special Plan Upgrading Reading. However, the opinions expressed herein do not necessarily reflect the position or policy of the Louisiana State Department of Education, and no official endorsement by them should be inferred.

119116

TABLE OF CONTENTS

PREFACE

The importance of staff development has long been supported by teachers themselves and by a wide ranging variety of educational agencies. Perhaps the greatest shortcoming in these efforts, however, has been the manner in which the contents of professional development activities are determined. It appears logical that the continuous need to update knowledge and skills should interface with the expressed needs and desires of those who will be the recipients of developmental activities.

In this volume the authors, from rich backgrounds of experience, treat several aspects of teachers' needs and concerns as related to the teaching of reading in the elementary grades. The text begins with the presentation of the results of a survey questionnaire designed to determine teachers' needs and concerns. The results of the questionnaire established the topics of the various chapters. These topics included: comprehension, readiness assessment and development, study skills, motivation and self-concept, and word identification and recognition. It is not the intent of this volume to be a complete handbook on professional development in reading instruction, but rather to provide information useful toward the effective teaching of reading.

Fall 1982   RJDS

vii

CONTRIBUTORS

Roger J. De Santi

    University of New Orleans

Patricia Edwards

    Louisiana Tech University

Roger Farr

    Indiana University

Patricia P. Fritchie

    Troy State University

Terry Lovelace

    University of Southwestern Louisiana

Larry Smith

    University of Southern Mississippi

Bruce Tone

    Indiana University

CHAPTER ONE

ELEMENTARY TEACHERS' NEEDS AND CONCERNS
REGARDING READING INSTRUCTION

ROGER J. DE SANTI
UNIVERSITY OF NEW ORLEANS

Teaching children to read is a basic and most important function of the school. The level of success of this function is frequently referenced to the extent and quality of both the preservice and in-service programs which are encountered by teachers.

The literature related to inservice activities in reading has indicated that preservice should be augmented with inservice as a means of maintaining and extending professional knowledge and ability (Moburg, 1972; Houston and Pankratz, 1980). Recommendations related to planning and providing inservice activities have been many and varied. Consistent within these recommendations, however, have been the suggestions that an active role on the part of teachers be encouraged through solicitation of their needs and concerns, participation in program planning, and limitation of the group size during inservice activities (Austin and Morrison, 1963; Adams, 1964; Andrew, 1981; and De Santi, 1982).

The present study was designed to identify elementary teachers' needs and concerns in the teaching of reading and to attempt to meet those needs. This study was commensurate with the opinion that, "Problems connected with the teaching of reading which are of primary concern to the teachers themselves should provide the nucleus around which in-service education is developed." (p. 20, Adams 1964).

Methodology

Subjects

Information was obtained through a questionnaire mailed to 160 elementary education majors who had graduated within the past three years from a teacher training program at a large urban university. Regardless of major area of study, all were required to take a nine credit, three course, sequence in reading education. The three courses included materials and methods in language arts and reading, materials and

1

methods in reading instruction, and corrective reading
techniques for the classroom teacher.

Procedures and Design

The general design of the project was a causal
comparative study using a survey questionnaire (Gay,
1981). The first mailing of the survey included a
cover letter and a self-addressed postage-paid envelope.
The cover letter is presented as Appendix A. At the
end of four weeks, a second mailing was sent to all
persons from whom no response had been received. These
mailings resulted in 57 (36%) usable questionnaires,
28 (17%) returned to sender, and 75 (47%) no response
whatsoever.

Instrumentation

The questionnaire, adapted from Pavlik (1974),
consisted of 40 reading related topics organized into
the eight subtests of: (a) the reading process,
(b) readiness, (c) instruction, (d) strategies,
(e) comprehension, (f) assessment, (g) the affective
domain, and (h) miscellaneous. A six point scale was
employed to rate the degree of need or concern the
respondent had for each topic. The questionnaire,
with mean ratings inserted, is presented in Table 1.

(Insert Table 1 About Here)

In addition to mean ratings, analyses were conducted
to compare item-by-item ratings and subtest ratings
with respondent characteristics.

Results

Item Analyses

In the place provided for the respondent's rating
of each item (Table 1), the mean rating of the group's
responses has been inserted. These mean ratings
indicated that thirteen topics were rated as highly
important (4.0) or higher. An asterisk (*) has been
placed following the mean rating of these items.

Breakdowns by grade(s) taught and primary area
of teaching responsibility. Additional analyses were
conducted to determine if there were significant
differences in item ratings between teachers of the
lower grades (N through 3) and teachers of the upper

2

Table 1

IMPORTANCE OF SELECTED READING CONCEPTS

The list below contains several reading concepts. Using the numbers for possible responses below, indicate on the appropriate blanks to the right the degree of need or concern you have for further information regarding that concept.

5 - Absolutely essential   2 - Of little importance
4 - Highly important   1 - Of no importance
3 - Moderately important   0 - I am not familiar
                               with the topic

I. READING PROCESS:

A.	Nature of reading	A.	2.981
B.	Definitions of	B.	2.698
C.	As part of the language arts program	C.	3.818
D.	As related to cultural factors	D.	3.111
E.	As related to dialect	E.	3.111
F.	As related to English as a second language	F.	2.660

II. READINESS:

G.	Factors of	G.	3.741
H.	Assessment of	H.	3.907
I.	Development of	I.	3.964

III. INSTRUCTION:

J.	Decoding versus meaning approaches	J.	3.830
K.	Approaches to teaching reading	K.	4.241*
L.	Uses of the teacher's manual	L.	3.113
M.	Uses of workbooks	M.	3.264
N.	Materials and equipment selection	N.	3.741
O.	Teacher made materials	O.	3.667
P.	Grouping: purposes and methods	P.	4.037*

3

Q. Development of meaningful   Q. 4.232*
   vocabulary

IV. STRATEGIES:

   R. Word attack skills   R. 4.463*

   S. Word recognition skills   S. 4.455*

   T. Study skills   T. 4.164*

   U. Rates of reading   U. 3.444

   V. Uses of oral reading   V. 3.630

   W. Uses of silent reading   W. 3.648

   X. Identification of compre-
      hension skills   X. 4.241*

V. COMPREHENSION

   Y. Characteristics of levels of   Y. 3.630

   Z. Factors influencing compre-
      hension   Z. 4.055*

  AA. Skill development   AA. 4.179*

VI. ASSESSMENT:

  BB. Terminology   BB. 3.000

  CC. Standardized tests   CC. 3.000

  DD. Criterion referenced tests   DD. 3.208

  EE. Informal reading invento-
      ries   EE. 3.259

  FF. Cloze procedure   FF. 2.792

  GG. Use of cumulative folders   GG. 3.000

  HH. Use of checklists   HH. 3.245

VII. AFFECTIVE DOMAIN:

  II. Motivation practices   II. 4.491*

  JJ. Improving self—concept   JJ. 4.554*

  KK. Encouraging recreational
      reading   KK. 4.255*

VIII. MISCELLANEOUS:

  LL. Parent participation   LL. 4.192*

  MM. Other_____   MM. 4.583*

  NN. Other_____   NN. 4.333*

Name (Please print)_____

Years you have taught _____

Grade(s) you teach: (Circle all appropriate)

    N K 1 2 3 4 5 6 7 8

Area(s) of primary teaching responsibility: (Circle all appropriate)

    Reading   Social Studies

    Language Arts   Creative Arts

    Math   Self-Contained

    Science

THANK YOU

grades (4 through 8) and between those who indicated
that reading was or was not a primary area of teaching
responsibility. One-way ANOVA of the rating of each
item by grade(s) taught revealed no meaningful differences. The lack of statistical significance
indicates that the needs and concerns of teachers are
the same regardless of grade(s) taught. A second one-
way ANOVA, item ratings by primary area(s) of teaching
responsibility, revealed several differences. On
eight of the items, the ratings of those who indicated
that reading was a primary area of teaching responsibility were significantly ($p < .05$) higher than those
who did not indicate that reading was a primary area
of teaching responsibility. The eight items were:
(a) reading as part of the language arts program,
(b) decoding versus meaning approaches, (c) approaches
to the teaching of reading, (d) teacher made materials,
(e) development of meaningful vocabulary, (f) motivation practices, (g) improving self concept, and
(h) encouraging recreational reading. These items
were listed in the questionnaire as C, J, K, O, Q, II,
JJ, and KK respectively.

Subtest Analyses

Factor analyses. While the questionnaire appears
to have content and construct validity, factor analysis
was conducted to determine if the grouping of items
into seven (plus miscellaneous) subtests was appropriate. Seven factors, accounting for 65% of the total
variance, were identified through a common factor
analysis with rotation to the varimax criterion. Major
factor loadings, the measure of the degree of correlation between each item and each factor were identified.
A loading was considered major if it was greater than
.30 in absolute value. The items corresponding to the
major pattern coefficients for each factor generally
corresponded to the pre-defined subtests in the
questionnaire. As a result of the generally uni-
dimensional nature of each subtest, ANOVAs were conducted for the subtests which paralleled the item
analyses discussed above.

Breakdowns by grade(s) taught and primary area of
teaching responsibility. Analyses were conducted to
determine if there were significant differences in
subtest ratings between teachers of the lower grades
(N through 3) and teachers of the upper grades (4
through 8) and between those who indicated that reading
was or was not a primary area of teaching responsibility. One-way ANOVA of the subtest ratings by grade(s)

6

taught revealed one statistically significant difference (p<.05). The Affective Domain subtest (subtest
VII) was rated as being of greater need or concern by
teachers of the upper grades. A second one-way ANOVA,
subtest ratings by primary area(s) of teaching responsibility, revealed two differences. On both the
Instruction subtest (subtest III) and the Affective
Domain subtest (subtest VII) significantly higher
ratings were given by teachers whose primary area of
teaching responsibility included reading than by those
with other primary responsibilities.

Discussion

Limitations

        Both the interpretation and generalization of the
results of this study should be done in view of three
considerations. It was assumed that the teachers were
capable of assessing and relating their needs and
concerns regarding reading instruction. Secondly, with
the exception of the two miscellaneous items (items
MM and NN), needs and concerns could be expressed only
as related to those items for which a rating was
requested. As only twelve persons responded to item
MM and only three to item NN, the possible effects of
this concern appear to be minimal. Finally, it is
assumed that the information presented in the mini-
conference discussed below was transferred to the
teachers' techniques and classrooms.

        Comparisons by Grade(s) Taught

        Division of the respondent's ratings by grade
level(s) taught revealed that there were no differences
among any of the 38 items. Apparently, teachers of all
the grade levels considered had similar needs or
concerns when viewed on an item-by-item basis. However, when items were grouped into their respective
subtests, the upper grades (4-8) teachers reported
greater need or concern in the area of the affective
domain. This may be a result of their pupils' older
age and longer length of schooling.

        Comparisons by Primary Area of Teaching Responsi-
bility

        Division of the respondents' ratings by primary
area of teaching responsibility revealed that there
were several differences among the items. In all
cases, including subtest analysis, the differences

7

were found because teachers who indicated that reading education was a primary area of responsibility responded with greater need or concern. With the exception of one item, the item analysis resulted in findings which paralleled the subtest analysis results. This parallelism indicated that teachers of reading had significantly greater need or concern for aspects of instruction and the affective domain.

Educational Implications

Based on the mean ratings of the items, a one-day mini-conference was offered to all respondents and other interested parties. The letter of invitation, mailed to all respondents, is included as Appendix B. As an effort to further publicize the mini-conference, flyers were distributed to possibly interested groups. A copy of the flyer is presented in Appendix C. The topics of the sessions included: (a) characteristics and factors of comprehension, (b) readiness assessment and development, (c) study skills, (d) motivation and self-concept, and (e) word identification and recognition. This approach was commensurate with the suggestions of others who have conducted studies in this area (Austin and Morrison, 1963; Adams, 1964; De Carlo and Cleland, 1968; Smith, Otto, and Harty, 1970; and Moburg, 1972). The mini-conference program, registration form, and evaluation form are presented as Appendices D, E, and F respectively. Those who attended the mini-conference rated its overall effectiveness as 4.6 (highest possible rating 5.0). This value represents the grand mean of the mean ratings given the first eight items in the evaluation form. The mean rating of each of these eight items follows each item as presented in Appendix F.

Research Implications

The factor analysis of the questionnaire generally indicated that it is worthy of further applications. Such additional applications primarily revolve about both extension and refinement of the samples studied into three areas. The first area would extend the sample to include secondary teachers. The second and third areas would include both elementary and secondary teachers and emphasize the perceived needs and concerns of preservice teachers and teachers with greater amounts of experience than those included in the present study.

8

References

Adams, M. L. Teachers' instructional needs in teaching reading. The Reading Teacher, 17, (January 1964), 260-264.

Andrew, M. D. Statewide inservice without colleges and universities: New Hampshire's quiet move toward teacher's control. Journal of Teacher Education, 1981, 32, 24-28.

Austin, M. C. and Morrison, C. The first R: The Harvard report on reading in elementary schools. Macmillan Company, New York, 1963.

DeCarlo, M. R. and Cleland, D. C. A reading in-service education program for teachers. The Reading Teacher, 22 (November 1968), 163-169.

De Santi, R. J. Trends and issues of diagnostic and remedial reading. Washington, D. C.: University Press of America, 1982.

Gay, L. R. Educational research: Competencies for analysis and application (2nd ed.), Columbus: Charles E. Merrill, 1981.

Houston, W. R. and Pankratz, R. (Eds.), Staff development and educational change. Association of Teacher Educators, Reston, Virginia, 1980.

Moburg, L. G. Inservice teacher training in reading. International Reading Association, Newark, Delaware, 1972.

Pavlik, R. A. An assessment of undergraduate preparation for the teaching of reading in the elementary school. (Doctoral dissertation, University of Northern Colorado, 1974).

Smith, R. J.; Otto, W.; and Harty, K. Elementary teachers' preferences for pre-service and inservice training in the teaching of reading. Journal of Educational Research, 63 (July-August 1970), 445-49.

LIST OF APPENDICES

Dear Recent Graduate:

Teaching children to read is a basic most important function of the school. The University of New Orleans and the Louisiana Department of Education are interested in determining the extent of your needs and concerns in the teaching of reading.

To help us determine these needs and concerns, may we ask you to take a few moments to complete the enclosed questionnaire and return it within the week. All questionnaire respondents will be invited to participate in a workshop oriented toward your expressed needs and concerns. The workshop will be held at the University of New Orleans during the summer session and will be free of charge to all questionnaire respondents.

Thank you for your cooperation and consideration.

Sincerely,

Roger J. De Santi, Ed. D.
Project Director

11

Dear Recent Graduate:

Thank you for responding to our questionnaire regarding your needs and concerns in the teaching of reading.

The workshop, oriented toward your expressed needs and concerns, has been scheduled for Saturday, June 26th at the University of New Orleans, College of Education, Room 310. The workshop has been scheduled as follows:

8:30- 8:45	Welcome and orientation
8:45-10:15	Characteristics and factors of comprehension - Dr. Roger Farr, Indiana University
10:15-10:30	Break
10:30-11:30	Choose one of the four small groups
11:30-11:45	Break
11:45-12:45	Choose one of the four small groups
12:45- 1:15	Evaluation and summary

The four small group topics and speakers are:

Motivation and self-concept - Dr. Terry Lovelace, University of Southwest Louisiana

Readiness assessment and development - Dr. Patricia Edwards, Louisiana Technological University

Study skills - Dr. Patricia Fritchie, Troy State University

Word identification and recognition - Dr. Larry Smith, University of Southern Mississippi

There is no charge for the workshop and ample free parking is located across from the College of Education.

I hope you will attend.

Sincerely,

Roger J. De Santi, Ed. D.
Project Director

12

Dear Educator:

WHO: You are invited

WHAT: Concerns and needs in teaching
                        reading
                        A mini conference

WHERE: Room 310, College of Education,
                        University of New Orleans

WHEN: 8:30 - 1:15, Saturday, June 26th.

PROGRAM: 8:30- 8:45 Welcome and orientation
                        8:45-10:15 Characteristics and
                                    factors of compre-
                                    hension
                                    Dr. Roger Farr,
                                    Indiana University
                        10:15-10:30 Break
                        10:30-11:30 Choose one of the four
                                    small groups
                        11:30-11:45 Break
                        11:45-12:45 Choose one of the four
                                    small groups
                        12:45- 1:15 Evaluation and summary

The four small group topics and speakers are:

Motivation and self-concept: Dr. Terry Lovelace,
    University of Southwest Louisiana

Readiness assessment and development: Dr. Patricia
    Edwards, Louisiana Technological University

Study skills: Dr. Patricia Fritchie, Troy State
    University

Word identification and recognition: Dr. Larry Smith,
    University of Southern Mississippi

INFORMATION: Dr. Roger J. De Santi, Project
                        Director, Education Building
                        Room 340, 286-6524

This mini conference is free of charge through the
sponsorship of the Reading Program of the University of
New Orleans and the Special Plan to Upgrade Reading of
the Louisiana Department of Education.

13

CONCERNS AND NEEDS IN TEACHING READING

PROGRAM

AREA	TIME	ACTIVITY
A	8:30- 8:45	Welcome and orientation
A	8:45-10:15	Characteristics and factors of comprehension Dr. Roger Farr
	10:15-10:30	Break
A	10:30-11:30	Word identification and recognition Dr. Larry Smith
B		Readiness assessment and development Dr. Patricia Edwards
C		Study skills Dr. Patricia Fritchie
D		Motivation and self-concept Dr. Terry Lovelace
	11:30-11:45	Break
A	11:45-12:45	Readiness assessment and development Dr. Patricia Edwards
B		Word identification and recognition Dr. Larry Smith
C		Motivation and self-concept Dr. Terry Lovelace
D		Study skills Dr. Patricia Fritchie
A	12:45-1:15	Evaluation and summary

CONCERNS AND NEEDS IN TEACHING READING

REGISTRATION FORM

We would like to know about you. Please provide the
following information.

PLEASE PRINT

NAME_____

ADDRESS_____

_____

Present Position and School

                    _____

                    _____

Years of Teaching Experience_____

CONCERNS AND NEEDS IN TEACHING READING

EVALUATION FORM

Please evaluate the overall workshop and the sessions you have attended.

A. EFFECTIVENESS OF THE WORKSHOP

1. The organization of the workshop was:
   Poor ___ ___ ___ ___ ___ Excellent
       1   2   3   4   5   X=4.59

2. The workshop objectives were:
   Vague ___ ___ ___ ___ ___ Clearly evident
        1   2   3   4   5   X=4.71

3. The scope (coverage) of the workshop was:
   Inadequate ___ ___ ___ ___ ___ Most adequate
             1   2   3   4   5   X=4.59

4. This workshop met my needs:
   Not at all ___ ___ ___ ___ ___ Exceptionally
             1   2   3   4   5   well   X=4.55

5. Were the workshop activities and information relevant?
   Inapplicable ___ ___ ___ ___ ___ Most applicable
               1   2   3   4   5   X=4.66

6. How much of the content will you be able to apply?
   None ___ ___ ___ ___ ___ All
       1   2   3   4   5   X=4.55

7. The amount of time devoted to this topic was:
   Insufficient ___ ___ ___ ___ ___ Most adequate
               1   2   3   4   5   X=4.37

8. Overall, I consider this workshop:
   Poor ___ ___ ___ ___ ___ Excellent
       1   2   3   4   5   X=4.66

B. DR. ROGER FARR, Characteristics and factors of comprehension

1. Had the consultant made adequate preparation for this workshop?
   None ___ ___ ___ ___ ___ Extensive
       1   2   3   4   5

16

2. Was the consultant skillful in presenting work-shop activities?
   Inadequate ___ ___ ___ ___ ___ Exceptionally
              1   2   3   4   5   adequate

3. Did the consultant distribute useful materials?
   None ___ ___ ___ ___ ___ Adequate amount
        1   2   3   4   5

4. Was the consultant's information current?
   Not at all ___ ___ ___ ___ ___ Most timely
              1   2   3   4   5

5. Interaction between you and the workshop leaders was:
   Poor ___ ___ ___ ___ ___ Most stimulating
        1   2   3   4   5

6. What was your general impression of the con-sultant regarding personality, manners and appearance?
   Poor ___ ___ ___ ___ ___ Most pleasing
        1   2   3   4   5

7. Overall, I consider the efforts of the con-sultant:
   Poor ___ ___ ___ ___ ___ Excellent
        1   2   3   4   5

C. Session Numbers and Titles

   1. Dr. Patricia Edwards, Readiness assessment and development

   2. Dr. Patricia Fritchie, Study skills.

   3. Dr. Terry Lovelace, Motivation and self-concept.

   4. Dr. Larry Smith, Word identification and recognition.

SESSION NUMBER 1, 2, 3, or 4 (Please Circle One)

   1. Had the consultant made adequate preparation for this workshop?
      None ___ ___ ___ ___ ___ Extensive
           1   2   3   4   5

   2. Was the consultant skillful in presenting work-shop activities?

17

Inadequate ___ ___ ___ ___ ___ Exceptionally
             1   2   3   4   5   adequate

3. Did the consultant distribute useful materials?
   None ___ ___ ___ ___ ___ Adequate amount
         1   2   3   4   5

4. Was the consultant's information current?
   Not at all ___ ___ ___ ___ ___ Most timely
               1   2   3   4   5

5. Interaction between you and the workshop
   leaders was:
   Poor ___ ___ ___ ___ ___ Most stimulating
         1   2   3   4   5

6. What was your general impression of the consultant regarding personality, manners and
   appearance?
   Poor ___ ___ ___ ___ ___ Most pleasing
         1   2   3   4   5

7. Overall, I consider the efforts of the consultant:
   Poor ___ ___ ___ ___ ___ Excellent
         1   2   3   4   5

SESSION NUMBER 1, 2, 3, or 4 (Please Circle One)

1. Had the consultant made adequate preparation
   for this workshop?
   None ___ ___ ___ ___ ___ Extensive
         1   2   3   4   5

2. Was the consultant skillful in presenting workshop activities?
   Inadequate ___ ___ ___ ___ ___ Exceptionally
               1   2   3   4   5   adequate

3. Did the consultant distribute useful materials?
   None at all ___ ___ ___ ___ ___ Adequate amount

4. Was the consultant's information current?
   Not at all ___ ___ ___ ___ ___ Most timely
               1   2   3   4   5

5. Interaction between you and the workshop
   leaders was:
   Poor ___ ___ ___ ___ ___ Most stimulating
         1   2   3   4   5

18

6. What was your general impression of the consultant regarding personality, manners and appearance?

Poor ____ ____ ____ ____ ____ Most pleasing
     1   2   3   4   5

7. Overall, I consider the efforts of the consultant:

Poor ____ ____ ____ ____ ____ Excellent
     1   2   3   4   5

D. Please add positive or negative comments:

CHAPTER TWO

TEXT ANALYSIS AND VALIDATED MODELING
OF THE READING PROCESS (1973-1981):
IMPLICATIONS FOR READING ASSESSMENT

ROGER FARR AND BRUCE TONE
INDIANA UNIVERSITY

Introduction

The broad perspective: What are we assessing?

Reading research conducted and reported since 1974, the year the National Institute of Education initiated its National Conference on Studies in Reading, has many implications for the assessment of reading.

A majority of the studies related to comprehension have focused on the relationship between reading texts and the reader's processing of those texts. Most of these investigations have been funded by NIE and have contributed to the increased understanding of how a reader comprehends what is being read. Although relatively little research has been directly focused on assessment, this increased understanding of the reading process is a prerequisite for improving reading assessment.

The Panel's Charge to Researchers

Ten panels were formed by the conference to outline research needed on reading in different areas. Panel 5 was responsible for delineating those research needs as they relate to reading assessment. Its broad perspective announced that if reading assessment is to become more useful in developing the literacy of our citizens, it needs to reflect and inform on all that we know about reading. The panel called for four approaches to achieving that understanding. Each approach was comprised of a set of related goals. In two of those approaches, the panel called for 1) analyses of reading tasks essential to functioning competently as a citizen and 2) analyses of the process one must employ in order to comprehend those materials. With a clearer understanding of the nature of texts that must be comprehended and of the process the reader must engage in in order to comprehend, one could more effectively consider the third set of goals set forth

21

by the panel: 3) the development of effective methods of assessing how well the reader applies the process to the essential materials. A fourth set of research goals set up by the panel underscores the practical intention of its broad perspective: 4) the translation of the findings produced by the first two approaches into recommendations for the writing and preparation of written materials essential to the functions of our society.

The Response to the Charge

An analysis of the research that has responded to the Panel's charge endorses its broad perspective, but the quantity of research and theory in the past eight years varies considerably across the Panel's four sets of goals. Most of the research emphasis in recent years has been on the second set of goals--developing models of the reading process. As modeling research and analyses of texts progress and can be related, the resulting implications should generate studies and development efforts which will lead to both better writing and better reading assessment.

Some analyses of reading assessment have suggested possibilities for diagnosing and measuring the reading process in ways that reflect the bulk of current theory; but most of assessment-relevant research has been concerned with the difficulty of using tests to distinguish between factors that are emerging as key components in recent models of the reading process.

It would not be possible in the scope of this paper to review in synthesis all the research and theory related to the broad perspective of the Panel. To attempt that for even the second set of goals-- modeling the reading process--would be both unrealistic and repetitive of other reviews. Careful on-going synthesis of what we are learning about reading as that understanding relates to the assessment of reading is needed.

This review is presented in major sections discussing the implications of text analysis (part II below) and the implications of recent modeling (part III below) while citing examples of research. Part IV includes recommendations that both summarize the implications for assessment discussed in parts II and III and capsulize some other issue-oriented implications as recommendations.

22

Any such review ought to be prefaced by the recognition that a genuine concern for developing effective reading assessment tools has not developed just as a result of the work of recent theorists and researchers. The struggle to develop meaningful ways to diagnose and measure the reading process has a history involving people who have been, it is assumed, well-intentioned and as informed as the research and theory of their times have permitted.

A Brief History

A brief history of reading assessment suggests that educators, researchers, and test-makers have historically attempted to find more valid and useful ways of assessing reading. Reading assessment is as old as the first mother or teacher who questioned and observed a child reading. The recent emphasis on the potential value of informal assessment in the classroom reminds us that formal testing is but one type of assessment and that to equate it with total assessment would be to adopt an unfortunately narrow perspective.

A limited outlook is promoted, however, by the fact that the history of reading tests is more easily specified. Although such a review covers only part of the picture, it does illustrate that the assessment issues brought into focus by recent research are not entirely new.

In 1913, Pintner reported a study which compared the oral and silent reading comprehension of fourth-grade pupils. Pintner's method of measurement was to ask each child to read a passage and then write down as much of it as could be remembered without looking back. Today, some researchers are stressing the necessity of understanding the relationship between short term memory and reading comprehension. Pintner's reproduction method is similar to the Silent Reading subtests of the Durrell Analysis of Reading Difficulty (1955), in which the examinees read and then recited orally from memory. It is also closely related to the comprehension assessment of reading miscue analysis techniques (Y. Goodman and Burke, 1972; K. Goodman and Burke, 1968, 1973) and the recent work of Harste, Burke, and Woodward (1982). The early emphasis on assessing the recall of what has been read is emphasized by Brown (1914), who discussed both the quantity and quality of reproduction as key factors in reading measurement.

23

Interestingly, the first published reading text, the Standardized Reading Paragraphs (Gray, 1915), contained no measure of reading comprehension. The Kansas Silent Reading Test (Kelly, 1916) appears to be the first instrument to attempt to assess comprehension. That test was not unlike current group verbal intelligence tests; and even today some reading tests still bear a strong resemblance to so-called aptitude measures.

Four early reading comprehension tests were the Courtis Silent Reading Test, Monroe's Standardized Silent Reading Test, the Haggerty Reading Examination, and the Chapman Reading Comprehension Test. The Courtis test (n.d.) was timed; each pupil was given three minutes to read as much as he or she could of a two-page story. Then the subject was given five minutes with the same passage broken into paragraphs--each followed by five yes/no questions.

Monroe's test (1919) was also timed. The examinee had four minutes to read a series of paragraphs. Five words appeared after each paragraph, and the examinee was instructed to underline the word that answered a question. The Speed and Accuracy subtest of the Gates-MacGinitie Reading Test (1964) used a similar technique.

The Haggerty test (1920) employed a vocabulary test and yes/no and true/false questions to test sentence and paragraph comprehension. The Chapman test (1920) had the examinee read paragraphs to find and cross out a word in the second half of each which spoiled its meaning. The Gates-MacGinitie (1964) and the Stanford Achievement Test: High School Reading Test (Gardner, et al., 1965) used a technique reminiscent of Haggerty's by asking the examinee to select one word from four to finish blanks in sentences. The modified cloze technique of the Degrees of Reading Power test of the College Board (1979) offers the examinee four choices for filling a blank in text scaled to actual reading materials used in instruction.

A key criteria mentioned by Brown but missing in these early instruments was "quality of reading." Depending on how quality is defined, one might ask if it is to be found in today's comprehension measures. Many current instruments do test inference drawing as a "higher level" skill requiring "closer reading," but none has yet incorporated the reader's purpose for reading and no one has devised a way of determining how what is read is put to use afterwards. Surely one's purpose for reading--which has received prominent endorsement in much current NIE research--affects the quality of reading, since many reading specialists now understand using what one reads as a vital step in comprehension.

Earlier definitions of reading comprehension as a "thought-getting" process tended to emphasize literal recall. In reviewing the 1934 Progressive Reading Tests, Dewey (Buros, 1938) argued that although the authors claimed to test interpretation and inference, the questions that attempted this were actually testing literal comprehension (p. 137). Spencer Shank had the same criticism of the 1934 Traxler Silent Reading Test (p. 139). Johnston (1981) argues, however, that from what we have learned about inferencing, much of what we have considered literal comprehension could be categorized as inferential (p. 27).

Early reviews from Buros' Nineteen Thirty-Eight Mental Measurements Yearbook deal with other issues not yet resolved. In reviewing the 1931 Metropolitan Achievement Tests (Reading), Joseph C. Dewey praised that instrument's attempt to measure inference drawing, but at the same time, questioned whether portions of the tests did not measure intelligence in lieu of reading (p. 131). Still a concern, this question has led to a few proposals to attempt to factor reasoning out of reading assessment (e.g., Tuinman, 1973-74; Royer and Cunningham, 1978).

Reviewing the Progressive Reading Tests, Ivan A. Brooker suggested that some items could be answered without relying on the passage (pp. 136-7). In Buros' Sixth Mental Measurements Yearbook (1965) Clarence Derrick claimed to be able to answer eight of nine questions on The Survey of Reading Achievement (1959) without looking at the passage (p. 334). This concern about how passage-dependent items are is still prevalent today. (e.g., see Tuinman, 1973-74).

The on-going need to arrive at a dependable definition of comprehension was succinctly articulated in the 1965 Buros Yearbook by Paul Lohnes' review of the Sequential Tests of Educational Progress: Reading (1963):

It is admitted that the tests measure a complex
set of reading skills, but no evidence is forth-
coming to support the contention that the chosen
"five major reading-for-comprehension skills"
are major components of reading ability, or that
that the STEP reading tests do actually "weight
these five kinds of skills approximately
equally." All we know is that a committee of
authorities agreed on this breakdown of reading
into component skills. With due respect for the
committee, it would be highly desirable to have
their judgments tested and supported by empirical
evidence. (p. 327)

Lohnes' comments exemplify the continuous concern that
motivates the search for the elusive answer to the
question: What constitutes reading comprehension?
Without a definitive answer, that quest has led to
the development of a multitude of reading comprehension
measures, which offer a variety of subskill mixes in
attempts to subsume comprehension.

The period from the 1940's through the decade in
which Lohnes wrote that review could be labelled the
"era of subskills proliferation." The intent seemed
to be to come up with the right set of skills in a
persuasive balance that would somehow capture general
endorsement. Across many of these tests, however,
single subskills were labelled differently. Some
tests had similar labels for the same skill, but tested
it with different types of questions.

A few years before NIE's National Reading Conference led to a call to define reading comprehension,
a list of all of the subtests from available reading
tests that appeared to measure comprehension came to
over 50 different designations (Lennon, 1970). The
tests that used these different labels were developed
as if there were a well-known theoretical construct
called "reading comprehension." It is this kind of
assumption that has fired the bulk of criticism of the
ability of standardized tests to diagnose--a concern
which has generated much of the researcher response to
the call for an universally acceptable model of comprehension. The recognition of this need, however, had
been jelling in educational circles since the mid
sixties around the writings of scholars like John
Bormuth (1970; 1973-74) and Schlessinger and Weiser
(1970).

26

It cannot be denied that the sophistication of test developers and test reviewers has increased tremendously. They have definitely learned to ask more probing questions about the theoretical construct of reading comprehension; they have been able to provide more sophisticated technical data on reliability, validity, and norming procedures; the editing of test items has improved dramatically. But the essential unanswered questions about reading assessment are still the same: We are still asking what reading comprehension is and how it should be measured.

Research conducted since the first National Conference has not produced the definitive answer, but it has informed effectively on the reading process and is now suggesting aspects of the reading process that are potential keys to understanding comprehension and how to assess it.

Implications from Text Analyses

We are beginning to generate descriptions of specific literacies required of readers

It is logical that if, over the years, it has been difficult to define reading comprehension, it has been equally difficult to define literacy. We are learning that both comprehension and literacy need defining in terms that can lead to improved instruction. The simplistic definitions of literacy used by the U.S. Census Bureau would have yielded little information on how to improve our citizens' ability to use language, even if the definition had remained consistent across censuses. (See Cook, 1977, Hunter and Harman, 1979).

Recent attempts to redefine literacy as "basic literacy" or "functional literacy" are helpful in that they bring us to the question: How well do our citizens actually have to read to function? It now seems apparent that the answer varies from citizen to citizen and across tasks for any one citizen. This supposition has generated analyses of the written materials essential to particular occupations and life tasks in an effort to determine what proficiencies they require.

Research of this sort has not been prolific, but what has been conducted has been so welcome that we have tended to accept it as definitive without examining it critically or bothering to extend or replicate it. The Adult Proficiency Levels (APL) study

27

(Northcutt, 1975) has been, perhaps, the most influential--at least among the general public. Questions about the setting of literacy levels, however, (Fisher, 1978) have arisen when its findings have been used to describe national literacy, and those questions have gone unanswered. The fact that the proficiency levels of individuals found succeeding at some jobs were lower than what the study described for the jobs indicates that while the study may be providing descriptive literacies for the occupations, those literacies may not be "functional literacies." It is not yet clear, therefore, exactly what proficient means in these descriptions.

It may seem impractical to recommend refinement or replication of studies like the APL study when the written materials for so many life tasks have yet to be analyzed. The fact is that there is an immense amount of work to be done in this area if such research is to yield trustworthy implications for literacy training, for writing, and for assessment.

Other researchers whose work is an example of text analysis as it relates to specific occupations include Sticht et al. (1973), Sticht and Caylor (1972) and Sticht and McFann (1975), who have done rather extensive analyses with materials essential to the armed forces; Mikulecky and Diehl (1979, 1980) and Mikulecky (1981), who have analyzed materials used is several occupations; and Holland and Redish (1981), who have analyzed strategies required to read and understand forms and other public documents.

The work of Charrow (1981) and Redish (1981) are examples of how linguisitics can be used in analyzing the written material of a particular arena. Both have discussed the literacy requirements of bureaucratic language.

Some studies of text have implications for a broader group of writers and readers. Studies such as those by T. Anderson and Armbruster (1981), Davison (1980), and Kirsch and Guthrie (1977-78) base their analyses on syntactic and composition factors that are more generic in their application.

As a collection, the work in this area would seem quite fragmented; but that is its appropriate nature. The researcher identifies and isolates specific occupations or tasks and collects written material relevant to them for analysis. In addition, the studies are diverse in terms of the analytic techniques used. The fact that it is a relatively new field allows the researchers to apply innovative approaches in their work.

At the same time that researchers are encouraged to examine new types of texts and to replicate and extend on each other's work, existing text analyses should be studied in an attempt to synthesize them. Such an effort might identify any text features that are common across types of text and that therefore do not recommend inclusion in a description of a particular type of text when defining its specific literacy requirements. This would set these common features apart from any truly distinctive features in a text.

Common features that could be cataloged and identified as highly relevant to a reader's ability to comprehend should be of particular interest for their potential in defining some sort of core literacy. As psycholinguistic analyses cross into the text analysis arena, types of literacies that have been defined can be related to or even translated to more generic features of the reading process. This should allow for the development of instruments based on text analysis that assess the generic process of reading applicable to all texts. It can be assumed that the study of literacies would do this and thus limit generic subprocesses across types of text (Erickson, 1978, p. 12).

Such a synthesizing procedure would quickly recommend a simultaneous study to identify techniques developed for analyzing written material, for until there is some relatively standard model for text analysis, comparison of studies will not be easy.

The potential implications of text analysis for writing and for reading assessment is obvious. Some of the existing analyses are of a critical as well as descriptive nature and do not fail to point up aspects of texts that make them easy or difficult to comprehend (e.g., T. Anderson and Armbruster, 1981). That text analysis ought to lead to clearer writing in the areas examined raises an interesting question: Would it be advisable for writers of text used for reading assessment to implement what is learned from these analyses before writers in general have implemented them? If they did, how well would the assessment instruments report a reader's ability to handle real-life texts, which presumably would be harder to read than the material on reading tests? These questions suggest the importance to test designers of on-going analyses of written materials--including periodic reiteration of the analysis of specific real-life texts.

The results of studying the written materials for a particular occupation or task can have implications for an assessment designed either to assess an individual's potential success with tasks involving the text or to diagnose instructional needs. Obviously, such assessments ought to reflect the schema domains, syntax, vocabulary, style etc. or the actual materials. As more texts are analyzed and can be grouped by commonalities, assessments that will pinpoint task aptitudes can be developed.

The Inherrent Relationship of Reader Purpose to Literacies

An emerging recognition of the importance of reader purpose is highly compatible with an interest in different literacies. Along with a reader's background and interest, it is the reader's purpose for reading that engages the necessary text. This same need assures that the reader will be motivated to use all the process ability at his or her command (McConkie, Rayner, and Wilson, 1973).

The recognized importance of reader purpose obligates the test-maker to determine ways to frame reading assessment passages with clear purposes (Reynolds and R. Anderson, 1980). The convincing indication is that a reader's ability to comprehend is greatly enhanced or limited by his or her ability to grasp how the text at hand answers to his or her immediate needs. And this awareness should have more real-life relevance than "I better do my best on this test"--a point which relates to concerns about the impact of test environments (Steffenson and Guthrie, 1980; Spiro, 1980).

When the reader's goal can be determined as simply the desire to learn and understand, the purpose-setting technique (for writers and test-makers) needs to relate the context of the material to some conceptual hierarchy that can be assumed for the reader. Thus test-makers need to stay abreast of developing refinements in schema theory (R. Anderson, 1977; Canney and Winograd, 1979; Spiro, 1980) and of any future studies which specify reader background in terms of specific schemata that one can expect for readers of specific ages.

In writing, considering reader purpose translates into audience awareness, a principle that has supposedly always guided good writers. Its exercise in test-making may be presently limited to using good editorial judgment as to what topics are of interest to and suitable for particular readers and are typical of text those subjects will encounter and need to comprehend.

The Challenge for Assessment

These concerns about literacies and their relationship to reader purpose suggest that assessment designers ought to be looking for the answers to questions such as the following:

How can test passages be selected and presented so that they engage the subject in a valid purpose for reading? How can items be presented so that the subject does not treat them as a very special and atypical kind of text reminding him of the test environment and thus setting for him an artificial purpose for reading? How can generic processes--yet to be more clearly identified as part of the reading act--be assessed and diagnosed without disrupting any natural purposes for reading that have been established?

The consideration of literacies raises other assessment-relevant questions: What types of literacies defined for specific life tasks should be represented on a test? In what proportion? At what levels? What kind of assessments will best reveal what educators need to know about how to develop their students' ability to comprehend different kinds of test? Will information about an individual's ability to handle task-specific texts be more useful instructionally than information about generic subprocesses instrumental to comprehending most texts? How literacy-specific should a particular instrument be?

The answer to the last of these questions is highly contingent on determining another purpose--the assessor's purpose for seeking the information. The more task-specific the need for information is, the more literacy-specific the assessment ought to be.

One need apply only simple logic to recognize that the definitive answers to most of these questions depend on the results of a great deal of future

31

research. Definitive tests that would reveal a
subject's ability to read one or more of a cross-section
of literacies will depend on extensive acceleration of
analyses of written materials and careful syntheses of
them.

Meanwhile, however, producers of assessments can
begin to apply what is being learned. As task requirements are defined effectively as literacies, the development of specific diagnostic assessments should be
possible. As common features across these different
types of text are identified, they can, it is hoped,
be related to subprocesses being validated in generic
reading modes. This, in turn, may lead to a definition
of a kind of core literacy.

A Related Consideration: "Learner Literacy"

An interesting argument arises from the assumption
that much of the reading that children do in the classroom is of a different sort than that they do outside
the classroom. It begs the description of typical
texts encountered in both places. On the surface, this
hypothesis would appear to suggest that by requiring
and teaching a literacy that is alien to non-school
activities, reading instruction in the schools is
presented as a relatively esoteric experience unrelated
to real life.

Such a line of reasoning, however, ignores two
obvious and qualifying facts: First, classroom
experience is an important part of a child's life and
comprises a significant percentage of a child's total
activity. Thus it is a major real-life activity for
the child. Society has determined that childhood
should be devoted to learning, not productivity,
necessitating the second qualification to be considered:
Instructional materials are apt to be necessarily more
heavily fact-laden and concept-complex than materials
the child encounters outside the classroom. In order
to handle this load, the materials may also tend to be
more syntactically complex. The facts and concepts
are also probably presented in frameworks more tightly
and logically controlled or structured than those a
child encounters outside the classroom.

This suggests that a student needs to develop a
kind of "learner literacy" to handle highly informative
texts. Analyses of written materials may inform us
that this literacy requirement is not unlike those that

32

are being described for some occupations or interests pursued by adults.

If we accept the existence of a kind of generic "learner literacy" requirement as valid, we will need assessment measures that inform the instruction of it.

It may be that text analyses will influence the writing of future instructional texts and change them in a significant way. If so, the same data should affect assessment materials. The argument for "learner literacy" just offered is not presented as a rationale for ignoring the obligation to wed instructional texts and reading instruction to the real world interests of children--by developing convincing purposes for learning specific things, for example.

We need to learn if there even is such a "learner literacy" and how it compares to the requirements of written materials a student reads outside the school.

How different are the texts used in the classrooms from those the child encounters elsewhere? How do they vary across different contents? Are they much like the informative materials the child encounters elsewhere and hopefully will be reading as an adult? Is there convincing evidence that children who are highly "learner literate" become more successful, informed, contributing, freedom-guarding, satisfied adults? If "learner literacy" requirements can be defined for students, are they so different from those of "real-life" literacies that children are led to eschew reading as an invalid, unessential activity? If such an attitude exists, can it be related to failure in school tasks or performances during assessment that is below their actual ability?

The possibility that the answer to some of these questions is Yes presents a particularly difficult challenge to assessment designers. How--in the limited time frame of a published assessment, for example--can the material to be read be presented so that it establishes purpose, involves interest, and yet reveals the child's ability to profit from classroom materials which by necessity may be uniquely more challenging than literacies essential to getting to and from school safely, communicating with adults, engaging in satisfactory play, and otherwise living and growing outside the classroom?

A major problem with concerns of this nature is

that we are yet forced to operate on assumptions. This fact endorses the perception framed in the four sets of goals calling for analyses to define the types of literacies required of readers and to translate them into recommendations for writing texts and the assessments that will inform on a reader's ability to handle such texts.

Hopefully, a brief review of these questions creates considerable anxiety over the paucity of research that has been proposed, funded, and conducted to respond to the incisive perception of such needed information.

Implications from Modeling Theory and Research

An emerging model of reading offers directions

The fact that the major thrust of funding since the Reading Conference in 1973 has been in the area of defining reading comprehension as a psychological process is reflected in the payoff. The emerging results of this emphasis demonstrate what can be done when a major commitment is made to a key set of goals.

Recent Validated Reading Theory Suggests an Emerging Comprehensive Model

The theories and studies responding to the second set of goals have come from different scholarly perspectives, none of which purports to be conclusive about its answers to the difficult question: What happens when we read and understand? What is most impressive--along with the quantity and quality of the response to the second set of goals--is the tendency among psychological, linguistic, and other reading-related specialists to take each other's work seriously. One result has been increasingly frequent interfacing across fields in what has become an exciting thrust toward discovering valid components that make up the reading act.

The bulk of the work completed between 1975 and 1979 is impressive, and the years 1980 and 1981 produced numerous studies built on the groundwork laid by those efforts. Anyone aware of the time it takes to conceptualize, conduct, and report valuable research will immediately recognize that this bountiful period in modeling theory and research came at the time one could expect a harvest from NIE's efforts in this area.

34

A synthesis of model theory in reading comprehension is a task for a scholarly panel made up of the various types of expertise that are contributing to the emerging understanding of the reading process. Meanwhile, Johnston's admirable attempt (1981) is available and is recommended reading for anyone in modeling research or interested in its implications for instruction and assessment.

Although Johnston may tend to see more structure across the various analyses of the reading process he reviews than can be endorsed with empirical certainty, his discussion of the compatibility of the work across and among researchers in reading, psycholinguistics, and linguistics over the past eight years is convincing.

Johnston's sensible, broad grasp of the emerging information leads his reader to believe that there is great potential for overlaying the analyses of the various perspectives to get relatively directive operational definitions. These, then, could be adopted to guide the development of measurement techniques to assess particular aspects of the reading process. The aim of such assessment, a synthesis such as Johnston's suggests, should be to yield information that matches particular instructional approaches, techniques, materials, and activities using the same analyses of reading that guided the development of the assessment.

One of the overriding contentions of current modelers is that the new analyses should enable us to learn how to assess the validated subprocesses it describes. The consensus argument is that most existing tests have failed to do that for three major reasons: First, the test-makers have arbitrarily selected the subskills to be measured without reference to any model; and in doing this, it is argued, they have also failed to adequately define those subskills. Second, it is argued that extant assessments of reading have not developed technologies to guarantee the validity of the data produced. Third, those data are produced by a limited number of items supposedly measuring each subskill.

Haertel's careful study (1980) of versions of standardized tests that are now ten years old tends to support this. He used nine comprehension subskills to examine items against large samples of extant data the tests had produced. He found that none of the subskills could be distinguished in his study but that there was a tight fit for the items overall to a model of reading comprehension as a "single dichotomous skill."

But Haertel's nine subskills were not selected from the skills the tests he examined professed to assess. Rather, they were a sampling of the types of subprocesses that research done after those tests were published tends to support. This raises numerous questions about the implications of this interesting study:

Having found in extant tests, items that he felt attempted to measure subprocesses endorsed as valid today, do Haertel's findings suggest that reading comprehension truly is an inseparable, dichotomous skill? Or do they reflect the contention that assessment item technology ten years ago was not up to distinguishing the subprocesses his study decided the items fit? Had he used the subskills billed by the tests, would he have found them distinguished? Haertel himself recommends extensive followup studies of his findings, but he believes that his study means that the tests he examined could tell us if a child comprehended or didn't--and only that.

The Immediate Implications: The Example of Analyses of Inferencing

Most theorists agree that the full, definitive model lies ahead on the impressive tracks of the past eight years. To illustrate how inquiry activities related to the goals of defining and assessing comprehension might now progress as interactive, let us deal with an example--a particular aspect of what is emerging about comprehension. Inference drawing has been selected here both because it appears to have potential relevance for instruction and thus for assessment and because it illustrates the need for extensive future clarification.

The danger in extending this example of but one aspect of the process being revealed is to suggest that inference drawing is being identified as a total reading comprehension model. While there is some indication that well differentiated types of inferences are the behaviors "upon which virtually all comprehension is predicted" (Johnston, 1981, p. 12), that is not the intended issue here.

In assessing inference drawing, one task for the

36

assessment designer will be to come up with the technology to validly distinguish types of inferences.
This prospect seems both promising and challenging
enough. Experimentation with the technology should
begin, using one or more of the existing taxonomies.
A second problem, then, is deciding which taxonomy to
use and whether any is both suitable and well enough
structured.

While the recently developed analyses of inference
drawing do not appear to be directive in any absolute
way, they are vivid enough to merit experimentation.
Work by Warren, Nicholas, and Trabasso (1979) and
Trabasso (1979) appear to offer some immediate implications to test-makers. The three classification schemes
developed by this team appear to be adequately enough
related to the construction of instructional materials
to serve as experimental assessment taxonomies.

It would be quite difficult, however, to use more
than one of the three schemes on any one assessment,
for the relationship across the different schemes is
not clear. Thus the experimental designer of assessment would need to decide if it is best to construct
items around Trabasso's definition using reader operations in coping with text features (1980): solve
lexical ambiguity, resolve anaphora, establish context,
establish a larger framework for context. Or would the
taxonomy offered by Warren et al. (1979) yield information more valuable to instruction? The Warren scheme
has four categories based on types of concepts (that
do not appear very exclusive of each other): informational, spatial or temporal, script-related, or
knowledge-based. Or would it serve assessment development best to use still another Trabasso analysis (1980),
which classifies inference by "protagonist actions"?
It is possible that a lot can be learned from
experimenting with item types for each of the sets
separately.

Continued research and thinking--including the
attempt to operationalize such schemes in assessment--
could well revise each of the above category sets for
inferencing--expanding and/or clarifying them. It
might suggest a still different perspective on the
analysis of inference drawing that would permit the
merging of the extant analyses into a single set. This
categorization would surely require a set of terms
other than any in the present analyses, especially if
it were to be broader--for example, incorporating an

analysis of reasoning into the analysis of inference drawing.

Johnston (1981) says the direction of research is now toward making the reasoning strategies involved in reading comprehension explicit. While he does not suggest that reasoning and inferencing are synonymous, he does acknowledge that they are each an inherent part of comprehension:

> While there is still some willingness to separate inferencing and problem solving, they are no longer generally considered to be removable from the comprehension process, but rather are considered an integral part of it, like the apple in apple pie. (p. 12)

It seems possible that in any taxonomy of reasoning, all classifications will involve inferencing and that the type of inferencing involved may help distinguish the classifications. It seems arguable that all inference drawing is some type of reasoning as well. If this is so, it might be possible to match inference types to reasoning types. It seems probable, too, that reasoning analyses will play an increasing role in explaining schema theory--particularly as classification as a type of reasoning is involved.

If reasoning is related operationally to the building of reader schemata, wedding reasoning to inferencing could conceivably bring these three key explanations of the reading process into the focus of a single operational perspective. Then, indeed, we would be approaching a definitive reading model. A concentrated effort to analyze reasoning, then, may forge the potential defining link between research on inferencing and theories of the schema persuasion. The major point of the focus on inferencing here is that research attempting to explain it demonstrates that such work is yet to be done, that assessment designers can play a role in the task, and that it is time to begin. Stressing that is not to criticize either the research of the past eight years or intelligent efforts to synthesize it. Rather it is to acknowledge the exciting threshold that recent theorizing and research has brought us to.

Space allowing, a discussion of other perspectives on the reading process would, no doubt, yield the same illustration of how good research and theory always reveal what we have yet to learn: A more encompassing

analysis might have selected Rumelhart's (1977) and
Rumelhart and Ortony's (1977) work with schema theory
and memory; Adams and Collins' work (1977) with schema
theory; Schank's work (1975) with memory and the
related script theory of Schank and Abelson (1977);
van Dijk's work (1977) relating semantic macro-structure
to comprehension, or Pearson's (1974-75) and Richek's
(1976-77) work relating types of grammatical structures
to semantics and comprehension.

The compatibility that Johnston reveals is a very
persuasive argument that the emphasis on the second
set of goals--revealing the psychological process of
reading--was no mistake. Modeling can feasibly
incorporate text analysis implications, and it is
beginning to produce the kind of direction needed to
improve both assessment and written materials.

Reader Background: A Common Denominator

The role of reader background is a key feature of
numerous developing models or descriptions of reading.
When the reading comprehension process is viewed as
one aspect of the full communication potential of the
human being (Collins and Haviland, 1979), background
is discussed as the reader's experience with communication. Searle (1975) proposes that the receiver
(reader) must use his or her background knowledge to
classify the sender's (writer's) purpose for communicating in one of five ways.

This perspective is related to analyses of metacognition (Baker and Brown, 1980; Brown, 1978), which
are, in turn, not unrelated to what might be called
"genre" type explanations, such as the script theory
(Schank and Abelson, 1977) or story grammars (Thorndyke, 1977; Stein and Glenn, 1977), in which comprehension is aided by the recognition of particular modes
of messages. In such descriptions, background develops
as the reader's awareness (at least subconsciously) of
what he or she is doing when reading. That is, as one
develops as a reader, he or she becomes aware of what
he or she is doing when reading.

Some models have dealt with background as memory,
which can function on different levels. Kintsch's
model (Kintsch, 1974; Kintsch et al., 1975; Kintsch
and van Dijk, 1978), which describes word concepts
deep structured by implied clauses, has the reader
relying on short-term memory when necessary to aid the
comprehension process. Schank's model (1975) has the

reader processing "nominal, action, and modifier" concepts in five ways: using syntax, concept categorization, and three levels of memory.

Clark and Clark (1977) see background's role as both a dictionary of word concepts and an encyclopedia of knowledge. Their theory analyzes the text/reader interaction as a process of considering propositions and identifying them as new (not part of one's background) or not new. Collins and Haviland (1979) stress the importance of teaching children to accept new experience that alters or contradicts what they hold as background knowledge.

R. Anderson (1977), Adams and Collins (1977), Rumelhart (1977), and Rumelhart and Ortony (1977) have all employed and developed the schema model theory in discussing the relationship of what the reader knows to his processing of text.

In all such modeling, Royer and Cunningham (1978) note the interaction between the reader's background knowledge and some kind of immediate or surface text processing. They call this basic interaction the "minimum comprehension principle." The immediate processing may be recognized by educators and theorists as any assumed activity ranging from letter decoding to using complex syntactic structures.

Sachs' contention (1967) that memory stores the message of text but not the surface structure endorses the distinction made by Royers and Cunningham; and in general, the theorists tend to separate surface processing from comprehension until it interacts with reader background (memory/knowledge)--as when Trabasso (1980), for example, stresses that background is essential to inferencing. Royer and Cunningham's principle appears compatible with most theories proposed and validated in the past eight years and with other analyses more specifically focused within either part of the dyad they see functioning in reading comprehension.

A Vital Contaminant

The emerging descriptions of how background figures in the reading process put a dilemma before the assessment designer. If background is integral to reading comprehension, measuring the process ought to involve reader background. That is not an unwelcome determination, since factoring background out of reading assessment is next to impossible. Yet back-ground must be controlled so that it will not account for too much of--or worse yet, an undeterminable amount of--the assessment results. The problem becomes clearly obvious to the test-maker concerned about the passage dependency of test items.

In general, the charge against reading tests is that they cannot adequately account for the role of such factors as background knowledge and reasoning ability and therefore are some kind of measures of intelligence--not reading ability. Thus they cannot, the charge goes, diagnose certain aspects of the read-ing act.

Johnston (1981) contends that the question of whether such factors as background, long-term memory, and reasoning ability can and should be factored out of reading assessment is now mute. It has been answered in the past eight years by research that can adequately answer: No! Comprehension is--or at least includes--those things. But that sensible retort leaves, as Johnston and others note, serious problems for assessment designers if their instruments are to reveal teachable focuses that are based on the best explanations of the reading act. Johnston's justified opinion is not reflected by theorists and researchers who, having helped describe the essential role of background in reading comprehension, proceed to concern themselves with how it can be factored out of reading assessment (e.g., Koslin, Koslin, and Zeno, 1979; Royer and Cunningham, 1978; Tuinman, 1973-74).

For assessment, the implications of the role of reader background--as knowledge, some scheme of concept structures, stages of memory, vocabulary/concept recognition, a base structure for hypothesis testing, Intelligence Quotient, or some combination of these--are both problematic and reassuring. To factor them out, as Royer and Cunningham appear eager to do, is, by the definition of their own "minimum comprehension principle," to assess something other than reading comprehension.

Meanwhile, we may want to control background as much as possible in diagnosing how well a particular aspect of comprehension is operating. At the risk of appearing to endorse an instructional emphasis that runs against the grain of the validated inherrence of background and meaning, the problem can be exemplified

41

using decoding of graphemes into phonemes. No matter what kind of item technology is employed to attempt to assess a reader's ability to perform this task--be it an artificial instructional concoction or a basic part of the process--the attempt will engage the immediate reader purpose of doing it to recognize a word. And the instant the reader becomes even word focused in decoding a letter, the reader is engaging his or her background in some way; for recognizing a word requires some kind of association of it to experience (say, having read or heard it before).

But it is difficult to design an item that involves only a single word in trying to assess whether a reader can read a letter. Will the item not have to ask him or her to distinguish it from some other letter? If so, it will need to put the target letter into a word and foil it against words containing other letters in approximately the same position that the target letter holds in the first word selected. Now how can the item distinguish the words that distinguish the letters without getting into sentence contexts? Even matching the options against a definition will be likely to do that.

Once sentences are involved, the item is assessing--to some degree--the reader's experience with syntax and/or semantics--not to mention any other background knowledge the sentence conjures. The higher up the process ladder assessment comes in an attempt to assess some specific aspect of the reading process, the more involved meaning--and potentially background-- become. As Haertel (1980) points out, for example, if one attempts to increase the degree of inference to be drawn by using a synonym in an item for a word in the text, one is really testing whether the subject knows that those words can mean the same thing.

In order to control for background, Royer and Cunningham (1978) suggest that schema theory be employed to write texts that fall within the knowledge base of subjects on whom an assessment instrument will be used. With a dependable analysis of what concepts people are most apt to know at what stages of life, this could be of assistance to test-makers, who have usually attempted to select topics for passages that will tend to have equal relevance to the experience of subjects across geographic regions, socio-economic differences, an urban/rural continuum of environments, etc. Common sense editorial judgment is used, for

42

example, to attempt to balance a passage that leans to a rural setting with one that leans to an urban setting at the same level within the same test form.

The same objective has led to the construction of passages on relatively esoteric topics that test-makers hope are not a part of the background of subjects for whom the test is designed. Of course, the test-maker wants such passages to be of high interest to the potential subjects, and that means that such passages are indeed selected on the assumption that the examinee has a general background that will make the esoteric topic meaningful and thus interesting.

At any rate, schema or similar theory relevant to reader background has yet to be translated into formulas that can help or assure the even or equal involvement of background when particular types of readers read particular texts. Text analysis can, and hopefully will, yield clear indications of the background that particular reader types ought to have if they are to succeed in life, but using such information in assessment still leaves us with the problem of distinguishing background knowledge from other reading process factors in reporting and analyzing the data produced.

Another step in this direction is the evolving determination of what "generic" concepts are likely to be developed by what ages. Such background can be moderately assured as the reasonable (or desirable) background of particular groups of readers by verifying its presence in curricula or life tasks. Once that is done, test designers can use any text analysis procedures proven effective to match passages to the assumed abilities of particular reader groups.

If test-makers were able to carry the recommendation that background/assessment be matched to the ultimate assurance that it is guaranteed across population, however, would they not also guarantee that what their instruments were assessing was background? Could they then overlay assessment techniques that could isolate other aspects of the reading act for diagnosis? How would one know that the background interaction assured did not lead the examinee to the correct answer to such assessment items?

The frustrating challenge may be to keep reader background in reasonable balance to new information that can be understood only if the reader can use other aspects of the reading process that background helps

43

call into play. As suggested above, that is what many test designers have attempted to do, using editorial judgement in lieu of having a system validated by research. But it seems worth examining whether assessment designed to diagnose particular aspects of reading comprehension can limit background in some way without producing text that has no appeal, thus validity, to the reader.

Johnston (1981) has an interesting recommendation that might facilitate the distinction of background's contribution to comprehension from other processing skills. He suggests the development of background measures. If matched to the content of a particular reading assessment and administered in a time period close to the reading test, the results of such a measure might be somehow deductible from the reading test score.

Meanwhile, it no longer seems reasonable to sustain a lot of grief over the realization that reading measures tend to reflect what we know about intelligence or that they appear to measure reasoning ability to a large degree. That is what reading includes, we have learned. Is reading, then, an act that cannot be separated into suboperations that can be diagnosed through assessment? We have every reason to demand assessment instruments that give us diagnostic information about specific aspects validated as part of the reading act and relevant to instruction (Anderson et al., 1978). Current editions of some standardized tests may perform that service to a higher degree than many theorist/researchers are acknowledging. The skills that they target may not be validated in the developing models; the skills assessed may not subcategorize inference as recent research indicates is meaningful to comprehension; the terminology describing skills assessed on standardized tests may seem archaic to someone on the vanguard of modeling the past eight years--but some of them clearly relate to aspects of reading comprehension in psychological models. That is not to say such measures are adequate in the light of the most recent research; and test-makers should be expected to incorporate the implications of the recent modeling as definitive validation and test construction time lapse permits.

Meanwhile, it is worth noting, the more dependable of the available instruments can tell the user that a child's instructional level, for example, is lower than his or her grade level (Farr, 1978). Some can report that this discrepancy appears to be due to a more specific "skill," such as the child's inability to infer between details in the text when the details are separated by a sentence or more of text. And a teacher can accept such test results as one piece of information (which is all that test results should ever be claimed to be) that recommends on-going assessment as to why the child is unable to make these inferences and how he or she can learn to do so.

Hopefully, subsequent reading assessment measures will include tools designed to focus on such subprocesses as inference drawing so that the resulting data will be based on more items than the assessment of reading as a whole process can present in the time period limited by the realities of school schedules and attention span. Admittedly, few such branching extensions are available as mates for existing tests; and that is another area that test makers can tackle immediately. Equally important, informal assessment of such processes directed by the standardized test's indication should be developed and taught to teachers. The teacher would then take the results of this assessment as additional information to be added to the results of careful, day-by-day observation, which is the most undervalued reading assessment of all! In this process, the standardized test will have targeted the teacher's attention in diagnosing for instruction.

Here, let us assume merely for the sake of argument that the role of background in the reading process is so inextricable that tests might never tell us anything more than a reasonable indication of how effectively (overall) a subject reads. Why would one want to develop, try to perfect, or use such instruments? Suppose then that such tests came to be based on validated theory and text analyses to a degree that almost everyone agreed that they showed the reader's overall ability to comprehend particular types of written materials that are accepted as meaningful for the subject's age, situation, or ambitions; and allow that such designations may be apt to relate in some realistic way to the difficulty level of the material.

What might a teacher do with the information such a test yields? The teacher could use this information to select written materials that are meaningful for the child and that the teacher can be sure the child will comprehend without frustration. Having the child read as much as possible is not an inferior way to develop reading.

Background and the Issue of Test Bias

One of the most prevalent concerns about the effect of reader background on test results concerns whether standardized instruments are fair to groups whose cultural experience contributes to a background distinctively different from that reflected by the text of a test. Data from the broad administration of standardized tests has tended to yield lower scores for urban centered and black populations and for readers for whom English is a second language.

That such testing can be politically self-defeating should be obvious. Levine (1976) charges that such use of tests is politically motivated by controls outside the minority populations' immediate environments. Whether this is true or not, the issue of test use is as fundamental to the solution of this problem as is the attempt to control background relevance in assessing the reading ability of such populations. This involves selecting the instrument on the basis of valid information needs that are clearly defined and related to reasonable and assessable instructional goals for the particular population.

Equally important, the issue relates to misuses of the resulting data. When might a school with a high percentage of Mexican-American children, for example, want to administer a reading test designed for the mainstream school population of the country? The answer ought to be obvious but, from the proliferated misuse of such data, apparently is not: Only when the educators need to know how individual students would succeed in a curriculum that adequately matches the test. Unfortunately, many students for whom English is a second language are forced to cope with such curricula, and the test could indicate appropriate levels of difficulty from which instructional materials written in English should be selected. The data would tell very little about the child's reading potential, and the test's overall demands might be so frustrating for individual children that any indications it gave for specific instruction would be overwhelmed by their inability to cope with most of the items.

The only possible use that can be contrived here for a school such as this to publicize the school-wide results of such a measure might be to convince a community that bi-lingual education and/or special funding ought to be installed or retained. Otherwise, the public use of such data is either stupid or as

46

suspect as Levine (1976) contends--a self-defeating exercise insensitive to the reality of the students' situation and inviting to the simplistic idiocy of critics who may be innocently incapable of understanding what the data mean (or more importantly, do not mean) or are not apt to have the best interest of the children or school at heart.

One of the concerns about test bias relates to what has been loosely called "genre" knowledge in this paper. In responding to assessment materials in standard English, lexical and other language "grammars" or "scripts" are assumed to be less available to a reader for whom English is a second language or to a reader who communicates in a distinct dialect. In addition, all the handicaps discussed here for special populations would limit a reader's ability to build a script for tests (test-wiseness). Powers and Sahers (1981) have compared the test-wiseness of four ethnic groups.

Test tailoring is being recommended for special populations (e.g., Royer and Cunningham, 1978), and at face value, it appears to make a great deal of sense. Special tests could be designed to assure a background fit for particular groups of examinees. Royer and Cunningham call for such research, which should profit considerably from the final reports from the NIE-sponsored Assessment of Language Proficiency of Bilingual Persons (ALPBP) Project (Rivera, in process). Cummins et al. have studied the relationship between a bilingual's two language proficiencies; and Tregar has studied whether the spoken English or second language reading ability is the best predictor of ability with English for persons for whom English is a second language. Rodriguez-Brown and Elias-Olivarez have investigated the communicative competence of bilingual children in order to describe it, and Hayes is doing this for Mexican-American third graders who are not doing well in school. Hernandez-Chavez is examining the writing of young Mexican-American and Anglo-American children as it is affected by early reading.

Other studies of the importance of considering the impact of testing on special groups include Doscher and Bruno (1981), Powers and Sahers (1981), and Linn, et al. (1980).

The development of tests tailored to special populations would probably need to be subsidized, for

47

the careful development of tests is so expensive as to
require that non-subsidized efforts be geared toward a
potential mass market. This problem suggests that the
development of informal assessment techniques for
teaching reading to specific populations is an attractive solution. Since the purpose of the tailoring
would be to yield information useful to instruction,
teacher-made assessment--including trained observation--
has a high potential for answering the need. The
background relevance of informal assessment conducted
in a specific setting is quite apt to be automatically
tailored to the individual assessed. All teachers
ought to be trained to make and use such assessments,
and teachers of special populations should be given
additional training on how to do that.

Tests tailored for specific populations would be
something like the instruments with the assured background relevance mentioned earlier as suggested by
Johnston (1981). And they could present the same
potential measurement problems. Having assured a high
degree of background involvement in the reading process
assessed, one is more reliant than ever on yet unper-
fected technologies that can isolate and allow the
valid diagnosis of subprocesses. Another requirement
would be instructional materials that tend to match
the background fit of the assessments.

And there is a possible issue that would be unique
to tailored tests except as they relate to say, teaching urban black children using materials written in a
black dialect. Johnston (1981) notes, if a test
matches a particular background, it may not always
match real-life tasks. Certainly it will be more apt
to relate to the real-life reading demands of children
growing up in a special culture relatively insulated
from broader arenas. But assuming that the child may
want to compete someday in American society at large,
should we be gearing instruction more to the communication demands of the broader arena? If so, assessment
will need to reflect that goal.

This is a complex issue that needs further
investigation. It generates a host of interesting
questions: Does teaching a bilingual child using
instruction and materials in his or her first language
tend to build background in terms of concepts and
generic "scripts" faster than teaching the child using
the second language? If so, will bilingual education
then insure faster growth if the child is taught from
English later? Or does the relationship between

48

vocabulary and stored concepts hamper the fluency of that switch?

Recommendations

Eight years of accomplishment delineate the need for more information

The third set of goals described in 1974 centered on the focus of the assignment: explore the implications of text analyses and modeling research for reading assessment. The discussions in preceding sections of this paper were representative of the questions and issues that assessment-relative research has addressed in the past eight years. Since they were selected for their potential impact on assessment, much of what might relate to the third set of goals has already been discussed. Thus the discussion of how assessment can respond to the work since 1973 will be presented here as recommendations that tend both to summarize what has been discussed above and to capsulize other relevant implications.

The recommendations below are lettered for reference convenience, not to suggest priorities; but the first three have been discussed first because they recommend research that might have more extensively complemented the research of the past eight years.

A. We need increased emphasis on analyses of existing instruments

Close analyses of assessment instruments are rare and should be encouraged. As the number of questions offered here suggest, there is a great deal to be learned from analyses of assessment instruments, especially when such analyses are crossed, as Haertel (1980) did, with extant score data:

1. Do reading assessment instruments now in use distinguish between the subskills that they profess to measure?

2. Do they appear to distinguish key subprocesses now being defined for the reading process when such processes are overlaid on the instruments as Haertel (1980) did?

3. How are any of these overlaid subprocesses actually labeled and defined on the instruments? What percentage of existing items can be overlaid with

49

newly defined subprocess designations? How do current
designations and definitions relate to emerging taxonomies of reasoning and inferencing?

4. What inferences, if any, are now required in
responding to items now classified as "literal comprehension"? How frequently do details highlighted by
literal items figure in making inferences required by
adjoining items? How related are the details highlighted by literal items to any reader purpose that is
assigned or that can be assumed for the passage on
which the items are based?

5. How can items that profess to require
snythesizing or evaluation be described? How do they
relate to any purpose that is assigned or can be
assumed for reading the passage they are based on?
Can they be reclassified under any emerging subprocess
taxonomies?

6. How well do the instruments reflect the
reading materials that the subjects they are designed
for encounter in their daily lives? How are the
difficulty levels or the text of the instruments
determined and controlled? Is there any consistency
in this across instruments?

7. What reading purposes, if any, engage the
examinee during the assessment and how do such purposes
compare with purposes for reading identified as likely
for the examinee outside the assessment environment?

8. What skill or subprocess distinguishing
purposes do distractors in multiple-choice items serve?

9. What professed or assumed subskills or subprocesses are distinguished by instruments using the
cloze technique?

10. How passage dependent are different item
technologies? Are there wording techniques within such
technologies that can assure passage dependence? For
example, does beginning an item that might be answered
from reader knowledge with the phrase "In this story
..." assure that the examinee will have to refer to
the passage?

11. What features best describe the informational
reader background affecting and effecting scores? How
do descriptions of the background engaged on assessments relate to the experiences of the examinees for

whom the assessment was designed?

12. In terms of background engaged, submeasures professed, types of passages and reader purposes, item types, etc.--are there existing categorizations within instruments that could be described as "domains"? If there are, how distinguished are those domains in terms of information reported?

This long list compiles just a sample of the questions that assessment analyses could attempt to answer. Such an effort could contribute greatly to the implementation of model theorizing and research by specifying how existing instruments do and do not reflect and distinguish aspects of the emerging theory. At the same time, it should provide the criticism of such instruments with specifics that could raise the state of the critical art to a truly constructive perspective.

B. We need much more research that analyzes written materials

Increased emphasis on and support of analyses of various types and life-task genres of written materials is essential to the explication of the reading act in two general ways:

1. Foremost, it is important that the descriptions of the literacies these analyses will produce impact on the work of the modelers; for not only should a definitive model of reading comprehension depict generic operations, but it also must be applicable to existing reading situations in which the model is in operation.

2. It is also important that the interlocked results of test analyses and model description impact on the writing of materials concurrently with their impact on the design of assessments so that assessments can report on the reality of written communication and yield diagnostic information applicable to instructing comprehension for real-life situations.

Reader purpose should, it appears, be a centralizing perspective in the analysis of written materials. If each such study accepts defining the type of materials and/or task in terms of reader purpose as a primary obligation, reader purpose should help synthesize, structure, and direct the overall task of test analysis.

51

Such research should also address questions like
these: What describes various adult reading competencies? Can they be meaningfully synthesized and defined
as a single competency? Can adult competencies be
quantified in some way on continuums so that reader
growth can be better measured and reported?

C. A comprehensive survey of test uses and
   misuses is needed

Much of the criticism of standardized tests is
fired by the misuse of tests that is so frequently
observed. The data created by tests are often mis-
applied by both educators and the public. The blame
for this is too easily laid on the test itself--even
when the test-maker has clearly warned the user
against it.

A thorough study of test uses and misuses needs
to be conducted and reported to all educators, media
personnel, and the public at large. Such a study
could help put a stop to misuse of tests resulting
from political manipulation (Levine, 1976) and from
ignorance. To do this, the effort must clearly explain what tests can and cannot tell us and on the
basis of this, recommend how they should be used.
Obviously, this study would also be able to identify
assessment needs that are not met by existing instruments and techniques.

Meanwhile, an analysis of attacks on extant tests
ought to enlighten test-makers as to what proportion
of the criticism relates directly to their determination to produce instruments that yield Grade Equivalents. The National Conference study group on
Linguistic Communication (Miller, ed., 1973) sighted
the problem: "We believe that grade level criteria may
often be more misleading than informative." (p. 4)

So ingrained are Grade Equivalents in the educational arena that explaining how they lead to misuse
of tests--and in fact have no legitimate use--is like
attacking apple pie and motherhood; and this fact is
the test-maker's only reasonable rationale for producing
them. Test-makers ought to be embarrassed by the
misuses of test results invited by Grade Equivalents
and be challenged to verbalize their rationale for
offering them. Presumably this would reveal any
possible way that they service instruction that has
been overlooked here.

D. The researcher should accept a share of the responsibility for the implementation of findings

As experimentation produces adequate assessments of highly validated reading processes, a major emphasis should be placed on effective dissemination of explanations of the reading act and how it can be taught. This includes reporting for different audiences. It should be obvious that if assessment is to be of use to teachers, for example, they must understand the roles that the subprocesses it measures play in the reading act. They must also be able to relate the information they get directly to objectives in teaching programs. Damon (1980) stresses the importance of educating teachers on the use of tests and test results.

Teacher preparation educators, methods text authors, and designers of instructional materials must understand the emerging definitions if teachers are to have the training, programs, curricula, and materials that reflect the process analyses. And the public, which has more and more control of curriculum, will need to understand and agree. It seems certain, for example, that the public will need to be educated about the distinctions between measuring product and process and how the latter relates more directly to instruction effectiveness.

How this translation of validated theory for public consumption can best be achieved needs to be determined. Each researcher and theorist, meanwhile, can assume a share of the responsibility; and this means each should become aware of the various dissemination avenues, the audiences they target, and how to communicate with those audiences.

All this suggests that an important consideration in dissemination is systemizing terminology when possible. It is important that the creative perception of modelers not be restricted in trying to explain mysteries like the reading process. If comparing it to an accepted model of something more concrete reveals connections not perceived or proposed before, adopting a metaphoric term from the more concrete process may be very descriptive and greatly facilitate the theorist in explaining the idea. A strict obligation to frame the explanation with existing terminology may, in fact, inhibit the theorist so that she or he may not visualize it in the first place.

But sometime in the future, it will greatly serve implementation if the common features of terms such as concepts, vocabulary, reader background, experience, knowledge, Intelligence Quotient, metacognition, schemata, frames, scripts, story grammars, etc. can be determined and defined with terms that help explain relationships between them.

In short, it seems probably that wide-spread implementation of a definitive reading process model will require that it be as clear and simple as possible. Applications of theory that require teachers (and students as well) to master a symbolic system in addition to language (e.g., Text-Mapping: Harper, Surber, and Smith, 1981) may be attractive to a few teachers and effective with their students, but such systems are apt to make only limited inroads in education.

E. We need to initiate an intense search for assessment strategies that can adequately measure the emerging model

Perhaps the most exciting aspect of the research of the past eight years is the promise that we may soon be able to identify specific aspects of reading comprehension with some definitive certainty. Meanwhile we need to be devising methods of measuring them, using the indicative definitions we now have. As Johnston (1981) puts it,

> ...we are approaching the stage of being able to classify items and item clusters with respect to the information they could yield. Thus we approach a position from which to select items which have a clear relationship to the structure of the test, the reader's prior knowledge, and the nature of the requisite cognitive processes. Knowing the characteristics of these item clusters, we should be able to generate tests which provide more, and more meaningful, information. (p. 69)

The response to this potential will be varied. Those who argue strongly that the cloze procedure is the technology that assures we are measuring the reading act should be experimenting with deletions controlled to reveal various types of inferences, reasoning, and linguistic, psychological, and psycholinguistic features of text and the reading process. Obviously any single deletion is going to cross types and features, and the cloze assessor is going to have to analyze the requirements for filling each deletion carefully, crossing the multi-facets of groups of deletions to yield some kind of gross distinctions.

Even as cloze is used to determine the suitability of specific material for specific readers, research is needed to establish percentages that indicate what is suitable for instruction and for independent reading. The percentage recommended by Koslin, Koslin, and Zeno (1979), for example, would place independent readers in material in which every tenth word is not recognized. They would use instructional materials where every fourth word is unrecognized. The potential for serious reader frustration seems highly probably in either case.

As domain referencing guides assessment experimentation (T. Anderson et al., 1978; Wardrop et al., 1978), various aspects of the reading act may be better isolated and categorized for diagnosis. Then different domain controls can be implemented in single assessments to test whether they yield distinctions among subprocesses.

Those who would rely on the statistically clean reporting potential of latent-trait theory will probably be engaging the technology of the computer and its branching potential to channel subjects to assessments of increasingly specific subprocesses.

Test-makers whose expertise is developed in constructing multiple-choice items face a challenge that is yet to be enlightened by needed research on the potentials of distractor control. Is it possible, for example, to pinpoint the reason an examinee fails to pursue a particular type of reasoning by noting that he or she frequently selects a distractor representing the same faulty line of reasoning?

Sentence verification techniques (Royer et al., 1979) will be tested to see how they can distinguish between levels of memory, which in turn may help distinguish subprocesses.

And there is, of course, the probability of the development of other, still undevised assessment techniques. It does not, for example, seem unreasonable to suppose that someday in the not too distant future, technology may allow us to analyze open-ended responses as effortlessly and nearly as absolutely as we score standardized tests. If so, schema theory and comprehension models described in terms of propositions may be the theoretical bases of such measurement. So should the work of Bransford (1979).

And, it should be hoped, future technology will allow us some way to assess reading comprehension in terms of what the reader does with what is read. From the perspective on assessing reading that values its real-life relevance, how a reader uses what is read is the ultimate guage of how well it was understood. Would such assessment tend, however, to dissolve the distinction between product and process measurement?

The prospects are fascinating, and--largely thanks to the research of the past years--it is possible to begin serious experimentation with assessment techniques.

F. We need a better understanding of the potential and limitations of criterion-referenced measures

Criterion-referenced testing can be highly effective in the classroom setting. Teacher-made assessment based on objectives set and defined by the teacher are, in the purest sense, criterion-referenced measures. The use of this general technique for broader measurement to assess grade-, school-, city-, or state-wide populations is becoming a widespread practice as an accountability system. Minimum essential exams, which have swept the country, are criterion-referenced measures. A benefit of this movement is the possibility that it should require frequent defining and redefining by educators of their goals, objectives, and philosophies.

The reliability of such measures, however, is usually undetermined, thus non-existent; and their validity is no more assured than the validity of a standardized measure. It is recommended that an extensive, nation-wide study be conducted of criterion-referenced tests--particularly those attempting to ensure the teaching of minimum essentials. A synthesis of numerous current studies of such measures would be a useful preliminary step in this study. The objectives of such a study could be far-reaching, since we know relatively little about how they are affecting instruction. Generally, these kinds of questions need answering:

What characterizes these tests? Do they measure
educational achievement toward goals that are carefully
defined and matched to definitions on the tests? (See
Moore, 1980.) Are they basically fact checkers and
product measures? How well do they actually match the
curricula of the sites where they are used? Do they
measure reading or reasoning/thinking in any recogniz-
able way? What reading skills or processes do they
profess to report on? Do they tend to yield much
diagnostic information? What kind of use do teachers
make of them? What impact have they had on teaching?

It appears that criterion-referenced measures are
being used to generate data that dictate a great many
educational decisions in this country. We ought to
know if they are that dependable. Moore (1980) raises
serious concerns about the use of such tests in
Florida, questioning how they were constructed, how
criterion levels were set, their reliability and
validity, and their use to fail rather than diagnose
and help children.

G. We need to understand the full potential of
informal assessment

In light of the current high regard for individualized instruction, the general distrust of standardized
measures, and what is being learned about how complex a
role background plays in comprehension, it is surpris-
ing that so little has been done to describe and
analyze the potential of informal assessment. It is
highly recommended that research energies and funds be
dedicated to answering questions such as the following:

How can the various kinds of informal reading
assessment that educators use be described? Where do
they get them? Are teachers adequately trained to
design effective assessments? If so, where did they
learn to do this? What kind of information do the
informal assessments yield? How do teachers use them?
How related are the informal techniques to instructional objectives and goals set by the teacher? How
do the techniques reflect the materials the teacher
uses in instruction? How frequently do such techniques
tend to measure process as opposed to product? Do
they demonstrate any widespread awareness of the
implications of current model theory or research? What
kind of technologies do such assessments use? Are the
technologies derivative or original?

Observation, the most informal and perhaps valuable

of all assessments of reading, needs to be studied too:
What kind of observation do teachers conduct? How
systemized is it? How often are students involved in
the kind of self observation recommended by Strang
(1970)? Are observation data generally recorded? Are
they synthesized in any systematic way? How confident
are teachers in using them in instructional decision
making?

The most important aspect of an extensive study of
informal reading assessment would be the synthesizing
and reporting of what is learned for teachers and the
teachers of teachers. But theorists, too, could see
how their work does, might, and could impact on
informal assessment.

H. We need to experiment with tailored assessments

It is recommended that the schema theory explanation of how reader background facilitates comprehension
(R. Anderson, 1981) be used as the basis for constructing reading assessments tailored for special groups.
The results of recent and in-process studies of test
bias, the linguistic capabilities of special groups,
and the role of both reader purpose and background
should be analyzed and incorporated in the development
of such measures.

I. We need to enlarge our appreciation of reading
as a form of communication

Theorists of reading developing communication
models should be encouraged to seek explanations of
how such factors as reader purpose, the reader's
perception of the writer's purpose, the mood and tone
of text, etc. affect comprehension. Such concerns
need to be better appreciated, and perhaps they can
be controlled to some degree during assessment. (See
Kingston, 1970.)

J. It is not too late to join the revolution

A change with impact equal to the industrial
revolution is in process. This is the age of the
computer, and more and more schools are experimenting
with computer instruction. Its immediate branching
access to a vast array of materials recommend its use
in instruction that would serve individual learner
needs; thus it can be expected to impact with surpris-
ing speed on our schools. It appears that students
avidly accept computer instruction and assessment,

suggesting that the format may dissolve any distinction between assessment environment and general learning environment. Industry is now putting that instructional potential to relatively sophisticated use.

This same potential can serve assessment, which is built into many instructional computer programs. The branching program, for example, can begin by identifying a potential reading problem, verify the diagnosis, and switch to more focused items to try to pin down the subprocess that instruction should attend to. This exciting potential is discussed by Frederiksen (1979). Haertel (1980) notes the relevance of such use to the latent trait theory of assessment.

The demand for computer software that teaches is so great, and the amount of material required to utilize the branching potential is so large that reading theorists who would have that software reflect what we are learning about the reading act need to act quickly. It is already too late to enlist in the vanguard of this revolution. Ideally the expertise of computer software designers, reading theorists, and educators would be teamed in the preparation of such materials. And assessment producers would be well advised to belie their conservative reputations and get involved. They could be the producer of the joint effort just recommended--just as large newspaper publishers are now investing in the computer technology that will replace their publications.

K. It would be foolhardy to slack off in the quest for the definitive reading model

One must not assume that without continued adequate support, the further development, refinement, and validation of the reading theory developed since 1973 will continue apace toward a definitive reading processing model. It is vital that this set of goals not be relinquished just when incisive analyses of factors within various models are defining and structuring their relationships.

59

References

Adams, M., and Bruce, B. Background knowledge and reading comprehension. (Reading Education Report No. 13) Urbana-Champaign, Ill.: Center for the Study of Reading, University of Illinois, 1980.

Adams, M. J., and Collins, A. A schema-theoretic view of reading comprehension. (Technical Report No. 32) Urbana-Champaign, Ill.: Center for the Study of Reading, University of Illinois, 1977.

Anderson, R. C. Schema-directed processes in language comprehension. (Technical Report No. 50) Urbana-Champaign, Ill.: Center for the Study of Reading, University of Illinois, 1977.

Anderson, T. H., and Armbruster, B. B. Content area textbooks. In R. C. Anderson, J. Osborn, and R. J. Tierney (Eds.) Learning to read in American schools: basal readers and content texts. Conference proceedings. Urbana-Champaign, Ill.: Center for the Study of Reading, University of Illinois, 1981.

Anderson, T. H.; Hively, W.; Anderson, R. I.; Hastings, C. N.; and Muller, K. E. A framework for analyzing reading test characteristics. Urbana-Champaign, Ill.: Center for the Study of Reading, University of Illinois, 1978.

Anderson, T. H.; Wardrop, J. L.; Hively, W.; Muller, K. E.; Anderson, R. I,; Hastings, C. N.; and Frederiksen, J. Development and trial of a model for developing domain referenced tests of reading comprehension. (Technical Report No. 86) Urbana-Champaign, Ill.: Center for the Study of Reading, University of Illinois, 1978.

Baker, L., and Brown, A. L. Metacognitive skills and reading. (Technical Report No. 188) Urbana-Champaign, Ill.: Center for the Study of Reading, University of Illinois, 1980.

Bormuth, J. R. On the theory of achievement test items. Chicago: University of Chicago Press, 1970.

Bormuth, J. R. Reading literacy: its definition and assessment. Reading Research Quarterly. 1973-74, 9(1), 7-66.

Bransford, J. D. Human cognition: learning, understanding, and remembering. Belmont, Cal.:
Wadsworth, 1979.

Brown, A. L. Knowing when, where, and how to remember:
a problem in instructional psychology. Hillsdale,
N. J.: Erlbaum, 1978.

Brown, H. A. The measurement of the efficiency of
instruction in reading. Elementary School Teacher, 1914, 14, 477-490.

Buros, O. K. (Ed.) The nineteen thirty-eight mental
measurement yearbook. New Brunswick, N. J.:
Rutgers University Press, 1938.

Buros, O. K. The sixth mental measurements yearbook.
Highland Park, N. J.: The Gryphon Press, 1965.

Canney, G., and Winograd, P. Schemata for reading and
reading comprehension performance. (Technical
Report No. 120) Urbana-Champaign, Ill.: Center
for the Study of Reading, University of Illinois,
1979.

Chapman, J. C. Chapman Reading Comprehension Test.
Minneapolis: Educational Test Bureau, 1920.

Charrow, Veda R. Linguistic theory and the study of
legal and bureaucratic language. (Technical
Report No. 16, Document Design Project) Washington, D. C.: American Institutes for Research,
1981.

Clark, H. H., and Clark, E. V. Psychology and language:
an introduction to pyscholinguistics. New York:
Harcourt, Brace, Jovanovich, 1977.

College Board. Degrees of Reading Power. New York:
1979.

Collins, A., and Haviland, S. E. Children's reading
problems. In R. W. Tyler and S. H. White (Chairmen) Testing, teaching, and learning: report of
a conference on research in testing, August 17-
16, 1978. Washington, D. C.: National Institute
of Education, 1979.

Cook, W. P. Adult literacy education in the United
States. Newark, Del.: International Reading
Association, 1977.

Courtis, S. A. Courtis Silent Reading Test.

Cypress, Edward J. Making reading achievement tests
    work for the innercity student. In C. B.
    Stalford (Ed.) Testing and evaluation in schools:
    practitioners' views. Washington, D. C.: Office
    of Educational Research and Improvement, National
    Institute of Education, U. S. Department of
    Education, 1980.

Damon, P. Standardized testing in elementary school:
    a practitioner's perspective on several signifi-
    cant testing and evaluation issues. In C. B.
    Stalford (Ed.) Testing and evaluation in schools:
    practitioners' views. Washington, D. C.: Office
    of Educational Research and Improvement, National
    Institute of Education, U. S. Department of
    Education, 1980.

Davison, Alice. Linguistics and the measurement of
    syntactic complexity: the case of raising.
    (Technical Report No. 173) Urbana-Champaign, Ill.:
    Center for the Study of Reading, University of
    Illinois, 1980.

Doscher, M., and Bruno, J. E. Simulation of inner-
    city standardized testing behavior: implications
    for instructional evaluation. American Educa-
    tional Research Journal, Winter 1981, 18(4),
    475-489.

Durrell, D. D. Durrell Analysis of Reading Difficulty.
    New York: Harcourt, Brace & World, 1955.

Erickson, S. E. Conference on studies in reading.
    Washington, D. C.: U. S. Department of Health,
    Education and Welfare and National Institute of
    Education, 1978.

Farr, R. C. Reading Survey Tests: Metropolitan
    Achievement Tests. New York: The Psychological
    Corporation, 1978.

Fisher, D. L. Functional literacy and the schools.
    Washington, D. C.: U. S. Department of Health,
    Education and Welfare and the National Institute
    of Education, 1978.

Frederiksen, N. Some emerging trends in testing. In
    R. W. Tyler and S. H. White (Chairmen) Testing,
    teaching and learning: report of a conference on

research in testing, August 17-26, 1978. Washington, D. C.: National Institute of Education, 1979.

Gardner, E. F.; Merwin, J. C.; Callis, R.; and Madden, R. Stanford Achievement Test: High School Reading Test. New York: Harcourt, Brace & World, 1965.

Gates, A. I., and MacGinitie, W. H. Gates-MacGinitie Reading Test. New York: Teachers College Press, 1964.

Goodman, K. S., and Burke, C. L. Study of children's behavior while reading orally. (Report of Project No. 5425) Washington, D. C.: U. S. Department of Health, Education and Welfare, 1968.

Goodman, K. S., and Burke, C. L. Theoretically based studies of patterns of miscues in oral reading performance. (Final Report of Project No. 9-0375) Washington, D. C.: U. S. Department of Health, Education and Welfare, 1973.

Goodman, Y. M., and Burke, C. L. Reading Miscue Inventory. New York: Macmillan, 1972.

Gray, W. S. Standardized Oral Reading Paragraphs. Indianapolis: Public School Publishing Co., 1915.

Haertel, E. A study of domain heterogeneity and content acquisition. Evanston, Ill.: Cemrel, 1980.

Haggerty, M. E., and Joonan, M. E. Haggerty Reading Examination. New York: World Book Co., 1920.

Harper, F.; Surber, J. R.; and Smith, P. L. Text-maps as classroom tests. (Technical Report No. 5) Milwaukee: University of Wisconsin-Milwaukee, 1981.

Harste, J. C.; Burke, C. L.; and Woodward, V. A. Children, their language and world: initial encounters with print (Final Report) Bloomington, Ind.: Department of Reading, Indiana University, 1982.

Holland, V. M., and Redish, J. C. Strategies for understanding forms and other public documents. (Document Design Project) Washington, D. C.: American Institutes for Research, 1981.

63

Hunter, C. St. J., and Harman, D. Adult literacy in the United States: a report to the Ford Foundation. New York: McGraw-Hill, 1979.

Johnston, P. Implications of basic research for the assessment of reading comprehension. (Technical Report No. 206) Urbana-Champaign, Ill.: Center for the Study of Reading, University of Illinois, 1981.

Kelly, F. J. The Kansas Silent Reading Test. Emporia, Kansas: Bureau of Educational Measurements and Standards, 1916.

Kingston, A. J. The measurement of reading comprehension. In R. Farr (Ed.) Measurement and evaluation of reading. New York: Harcourt, Brace & World, 1970.

Kintsch, W. The representation of meaning in memory. Hillsdale, N. J.: Erlbaum, 1974.

Kintsch, W.; Kozminsky, E.; Streby, W. J.; McKoon, G.; and Keenan, J. M. Comprehension and recall of text as a function of content variables. Journal of Verbal Learning and Verbal Behavior, 1975, 14, 196-214.

Kintsch, W., and van Dijk, T. A. Toward a model of text comprehension and production. Psychological Review, 1978, 85, 363-394.

Kirsch, I., and Guthrie, J. T. The concept and measurement of functional literacy. Reading Research Quarterly, 1977-78, 13(4), 485-507.

Koslin, B. L.; Koslin, S.; and Zeno, S. Towards an effectiveness measure in reading. In R. W. Tyler and S. H. White (Chairmen) Testing, teaching and learning: report of a conference on research in testing, August 17-26, 1978. Washington, D. C.: National Institute of Education, 1979.

Lennon, R. T. What can be measured? In R. Farr (Ed.) Measurement and evaluation of reading. New York: Harcourt, Brace & World, 1970.

Levine, Murray. The academic achievement test: its historical context and social functions. American Psychologist, March 1976, 228-238.

Linn, R. L.; Levine, M. V.; Hastings, C. N.; and
    Wardrop, J. L. An investigation of item bias in
    a test of reading comprehension. (Technical
    Report No. 163) Urbana-Champaign, Ill.: Center
    for the Study of Reading, University of Illinois,
    1980.

McConkie, G. W.; Rayner, K.; and Wilson, S. J.
    Experimental manipulation of reading strategies.
    Journal of Reading Psychology, 1973, 65, 1-8.

Mikulecky, L. J. Job literacy: the relationship
    between school preparation and work place actu-
    ality. (Final Report to NIE) Bloomington, Ind.:
    Reading Research Center, Department of Reading,
    Indiana University, 1981.

Mikulecky, L. J., and Diehl, W. Job literacy: a
    study of literacy demands, attitudes, and strat-
    egies in a cross-section of occupations.
    Bloomington, Ind.: Reading Research Center,
    Department of Reading, Indiana University, 1980.

Mikulecky, L. J., and Diehl, W. Literacy requirements
    in business and industry. Bloomington, Ind.:
    Reading Research Center, Department of Reading,
    Indiana University, 1979.

Miller, G. A. (Ed.) Linguistic communication: perspec-
    tives for research. Newark, Del.: International
    Reading Association, 1973.

Monroe, W. S. Monroe's Standardized Silent Reading
    Test. Indianapolis: Bobbs-Merrill, 1919.

Moore, W. Florida's standardized testing program: a
    tool or a weapon? In C. B. Stalford (Ed.) Testing
    and evaluation in schools: practitioners' views.
    Washington, D. C.: Office of Educational Research
    and Improvement, National Institute of Education,
    U. S. Department of Education, 1980.

Northcutt, N. Adult functional competency: a summary.
    Austin, Tex.: University of Texas at Austin,
    1975.

Pearson, P. D. The effects of grammatical complexity
    on children's comprehension, recall, and concep-
    tion of certain semantic relations. Reading
    Research Quarterly, 1974-75, 10(2), 155-192.

Pintner, Rudolf. Oral and silent reading of fourth grade pupils. Journal of Educational Psychology, 1913, 4, 333-337.

Powers, S., and Sahers, D. An investigation of ethnic group differences in testwiseness at the third, fifth, and seventh grade. Paper presented at the annual meeting of the American Educational Research Association, Los Angeles, Cal., April 13-17, 1981.

Redish, J. C. The language of the bureaucracy. (Document Design Project) Washington, D. C.: American Institutes for Research, 1981.

Reynolds, R. E., and Anderson, R. C. Influence of questions on the allocation of attention during reading. (Technical Report No. 183) Urbana-Champaign, Ill.: Center for the Study of Reading, University of Illinois, 1980.

Richek, M. A. Reading comprehension of anaphoric forms in varying linguistic contexts. Reading Research Quarterly, 1976-77, 12(2), 145-165.

Rivera, C. (Contact person) Assessment of Language Proficiency of Bilingual Persons (ALPBP) project: Research Component Progress Report No. 2, Inter-America Research Associates (703/522-0870), February 23, 1981.

Royer, J. M., and Cunningham, D. J. On the theory and measurement of reading comprehension. (Technical Report No. 91) Urbana-Champaign, Ill.: Center for the Study of Reading, University of Illinois, 1978.

Royer, J. M.; Hastings, C. N.; and Hook, C. A sentence verification technique for measuring reading comprehension. (Technical Report No. 137) Urbana-Champaign, Ill.: Center for the Study of Reading, University of Illinois, 1979.

Rumelhart, D. E. Toward an interactive model of reading. In S. Dornic (Ed.) Attention and performance (Vol. 6). Hillsdale, N. J.: Erlbaum, 1977.

Rumelhart, D. E. and Ortony, A. The representation of knowledge in memory. In R. C. Anderson et al. (Eds.) Schooling and the acquisition of knowledge. Hillsdale, N. J.: Erlbaum, 1977.

Sachs, J. S. Recognition memory for syntactic and semantic aspects of connected discourse. Perception and Psychophysics, 1967, 2, 437-442.

Schlesinger, I. M., and Weiser, Zehavit. A facet design for tests of reading comprehension. Reading Research Quarterly, Summer 1970, 5(4), 566-580.

Searl, J. R. A taxonomy of illocutionary acts. In K. Gunderson (Ed.) Minnesota Studies in the Philosophy of Language. Minneapolis: University of Minnesota Press, 1975.

Schank, R. C. Conceptual dependency: a theory of natural language understanding. Cognitive Psychology, 1972, 3, 552-631.

Schank, R. C. The structure of episodes in memory. In D. G. Bobrow and A. Collins (Eds.) Representation and understanding: studies in cognitive science. New York: Academic Press, 1975.

Schank, R. C., and Abelson, R. P. Scripts, plans, goals and understanding. Hillsdale, N. J.: Erlbaum, 1977.

Spiro, R. J. Schema theory and reading comprehension: new directions. (Technical Report No. 191) Urbana-Champaign, Ill.: Center for the Study of Reading, University of Illinois, 1980.

Steffensen, M. S., and Guthrie, L. F. Effects of situation on the verbalization of black inner-city children. (Technical Report No. 180) Urbana-Champaign, Ill.: Center for the Study of Reading, University of Illinois, 1980.

Stein, N. L., and Glenn, C. G. An analysis of story comprehension in elementary school children. In R. O. Freedle (Ed.) Multidisciplinary approaches to discourse comprehension. Hillsdale, N. J.: Ablex, 1977.

Sticht, T. G., and Caylor, J. S. Development and evaluation of job reading task tests. Journal of Reading Behavior, Fall 1972, 4, 29-50.

Sticht, T. G.; Caylor, J. S.; Hern, R. P.; and Fox, L. C. Project REALISTIC: determination of adult functional literacy skill levels. Reading Research Quarterly, Spring 1973, 7(3), 424-465.

Sticht, T. G., and McFann, H. H. Reading requirements for career entry. In D. M. Nielsen and H. F. Hjelm (Eds.) Reading and career education. Perspectives in Reading No. 19 Newark, Del.: International Reading Association, 1975.

Strang, R. Evaluation of development in and through reading. In R. Farr (Ed.) Measurement and evaluation of reading. New York: Harcourt, Brace & World, 1970.

Trabasso, T. On the making of inferences during reading and their assessment. (Technical Report No. 157) Urbana-Champaign, Ill.: Center for the Study of Reading, University of Illinois, 1980.

Thorndyke, P. W. Cognitive structures in comprehension and memory of narrative discourse. Cognitive Psychology, 1977, 9, 77-110.

Tuinman, J. J. Determining the passage dependency of comprehension questions in 5 major tests. Reading Research Quarterly, 1973-74, 9(2), 206-223.

van Dijk, T. A. Semantic macro-structures and knowledge frames in discourse comprehension. In M. A. Just and P. A. Carpenter (Eds.) Cognitive processes in comprehension. Hillsdale, N. J.: Erlbaum, 1977.

Warren, W. H.; Nicholas, D. N.; and Trabasso, T. Event chains and inferences in understanding narratives. In R. O. Freedle (Ed.) New directions in discourse processing: advances in discourse processes (Vol. 2) Hillsdale, N. J.: Erlbaum, 1979.

CHAPTER THREE

MOTIVATION AND SELF-CONCEPT
RELATED TO READING ACHIEVEMENT

TERRY LOVELACE
UNIVERSITY OF SOUTHWESTERN LOUISIANA

Introduction

When classroom teachers of reading are asked for
topics for inservice programs designed to help them
improve students' academic achievement, presentations
related to self-concept and/or motivation are often
requested. The number of these requests appears to
indicate that teachers believe a strong positive
correlation exists between students' academic achievement and their motivation and/or self-concept. A
review of the literature reveals definitions for both
affective terms, factors related to motivation and
self-concept, and methods of measuring these constructs
as they relate to reading achievement. Practical
suggestions resulting from both empirical research and
pragmatic classroom observation were gleaned from the
review of the literature and are delineated in the
last part of this chapter.

Definition of Motivation

Motivation as it relates to reading achievement
can be defined as the processes involved in arousing,
directing, and sustaining specific reading behaviors
(Ball, 1977). Recognize, however, that motivation is
a hypothetical construct, an inference based on direct
observations of students' behaviors. Psychologists
can only describe the behavior resulting from motivation; they cannot provide explanations of the cognitive
processes involved.

Reading educators frequently express frustration
resulting from students' "lack of motivation" in their
classrooms. A more accurate appraisal would be:
"These students are not motivated to learn with me at
this time." Teachers cannot motivate students; they
can only provide a learning environment so structured
that children are stimulated to learn to read and to
develop lifelong reading habits.

Precautionary notes:

1. The best predictor of reading achievement is

reading ability. While motivation plays an important part in acquiring the reading skills, a highly-motivated child with severe skill deficiencies may perform more poorly than a less-motivated child who has mastered more of the reading skills. Again, the best predictor of achievement is ability.

2. Teachers should carefully consider the values involved as they attempt to motivate: they are helping to mold children's personalities, affecting the kinds of people these children become, and helping to determine the kind of society they will live in.

Definition of Self-Concept

Self-concept is defined as "the totality of the individual's thoughts and feelings having reference to himself as an object" (Rosenberg, 1977, p. 7). Self-concept is the picture of the self--not what the self is, or is capable of doing in reality, but what a person thinks he is or is capable of doing. Again, self-concept is a hypothetical construct, measurable only through observations of students' behaviors.

Both self-concept and motivation are frequently spoken of in global terms. However, a child's self-concept and motivation to achieve in reading may be very different from his self-concept and motivation to achieve in physical education classes. For the purposes of this paper, and based on the results of research in this area, motivation will refer to academic motivation in the area of reading, while self-concept will refer to self-concept related to reading achievement.

Factors Affecting Reader's Motivation and Self-concept

Two areas have attracted much more attention recently in reading research in Great Britain--reading comprehension and the importance of self-concept and/or motivation (Goodacre, 1980). The same areas are frequently cited in the United States by reading educators completing needs assessment instruments for future staff development and inservice programs. Before such programs are instituted, the factors underlining these areas and contributing to their complexity should be examined. Reading educators agree on the complex nature of the process of comprehension, yet fail to take into account the multiplicity of factors underlying motivation and self-concept.

Both motivation and self-concept must be rigorously

70

defined before educators attempt to quantitatively
measure these factors and try to promote positive
growth. When researchers attempted to measure self-
concept and motivation in a global way, and then to
correlate achievement with these affective constructs,
they failed to obtain the results teachers expected.
For example, Wheeler and Reilly (1980) failed to
demonstrate a positive relationship between general,
overall self-concept and academic achievement in the
areas of mathematics and reading. An investigation
by Whaley (1979) revealed that a child's global esteem
is not significantly related to reading gains in
individual remedial reading instruction. Furthermore,
a study of the self-concept of intellectually superior
children (Neufeld and Cozac, 1980) revealed no
significant relationship between overall self-concept
and reading comprehension. However, the proven
relationship between intelligence and reading comprehension suggests that if the investigators had
measured reading self-concept alone, a high correlation
would have emerged, since most academically gifted
children read very well, and experience a great deal
of success with reading-related activities.

Gose, Wooden, and Muller (1980) present evidence
suggesting that investigators wishing to control for
self-concept in studies of academic achievement should
use measures of self-concept that are specifically
reflective of academic success in the content area
being investigated. For instance, reading achievement
was found to relate closely to academic self-concept
but not to physical maturity, peer relationships, and
school adaptiveness self-concepts (Gose, 1980), while
school self-esteem was found to be significantly
associated with test anxiety and reading and mathematics
achievement (Shoemaker, 1980).

Despite research which focuses on self-concept
and motivation specific to reading achievement (which
does correlate highly with student performance) the
best predictor of future reading achievement is still
previous reading achievement. This hypothesis is
supported by Lehn (1980), who investigated a sample of
eleventh grade students from four different ethnic
backgrounds, and found reading achievement test scores
to be more valid predictors of academic success in
reading than was academic self-concept.

Factors Affecting Motivation

Academic motivation related to reading achievement

71

can be affected by many factors, the most important of which are discussed in the following paragraphs:

Curiosity. Curiosity about knowledge (termed epistemic curiosity) is one factor affecting reading motivation. Torrence (1967) links curiosity to creativity, and suggests that curiosity is related positively to IQ, and inversely to anxiety. A child's level of curiosity affects his desire to learn to read and to read to learn.

Anxiety. Studies reveal a negative relationship between anxiety and academic performance. For any task at a given level of complexity, there is a level of anxiety that is optional for performance at that task (Yerkes-Dodson Law). Beyond that level the learner must direct energy from learning to handling his tension and anxiety. Consequently, he does not have as much energy to devote to the reading task.

Attitude. Attitudes are "enduring systems of positive or negative evaluations, emotional feelings, and pro or con action tendencies with respect to social objects" (Krech, Crutchfield, and Ballochey, 1962, p. 139).

A six-year study of sex differences in affective development and reading achievement (Yarborough and Johnson, 1980) revealed girls have more positive attitudes toward school, reading and language arts, classmates and teachers. In other words, they tend to feel better about themselves. The investigators suggest further research to determine precisely the causes and the consequences of the apparent affective disadvantages of boys detected in this study, since the investigators suspect that attitude and not innate ability, is responsible for the differences in reading performance of males and females. It is not, suggest Yarborough and Johnson, that boys are congenitally poor readers, it is that their negative attitudes interfere with normal reading achievement.

Interests. Interests are patterns of choice among alternatives, which demonstrate high stability over time and do not appear to result from external pressures (Rust, 1977).

Factors influencing reading interest include:

1. personal determinants: sex, age, intelligence,

72

reading ability, attitude and psychological needs;

2. institutional determinants: availability of books; socioeconomic status and ethnic background; peer, parent, and teacher influences; and TV and movies;

3. illustrations;

4. difficulty of level of reading material (Harris and Sipay, 1980).

Needs. Usually expressed in terms of Maslow's needs hierarchy, (Maslow, 1968), needs are defined (moving from lowest to highest) as physiological, safety, belongingness and love, esteem, self-actualization, and desire to know and understand. If the student's needs on the lowest levels are not met, it is unlikely that he/she will develop the highest level need, the desire to know and understand. A hungry child concentrates his attention on filling his stomach, not his mind.

Stimulation. Stimulation includes establishing anticipatory sets for learning, providing a variety of learning methodology and materials, sequencing and asking several types of questions during discussions led by the teacher, employing audiovisuals to help reinforce key points, etc. Cramer and Schubert (1979) raise doubts about the effectiveness of reading skills management systems, with their system of fragmenting reading into drill on isolated skills. They suggest that sustained motivation and stimulation are more important than an overly-structured skills management system.

Positive orientation toward school learning. This involves persistence (including attention span and drive to complete the assigned task), level of aspiration, positive academic (reading) self-concept, and positive feelings about past performance at reading activities. Some researchers suggest, and many teachers agree, that the reading problem facing many moderately-deficient readers is not so much skill deficiency as it is negative attitude toward reading (Doggett, 1979).

Butkowsky and Willows (1980) discovered poor readers' low self-concept in reading was characterized by their low initial expectancies of success on a given

73

task in reading. The poor readers felt their failure and reacted to it more strongly than good readers. The confidence of poor readers is more easily shaken when failure occurs. Poor readers demonstrated markedly lower persistence in the face of difficulty, and took less personal responsibility for their failure. By helping poor readers modify what they say to themselves about their reading performance, teachers may potentially increase students' motivation, persistence and expectancy of success in reading. Some training should be provided for remedial reading students on how to handle failure successfully, so that they maintain a positive attitude toward school learning.

Need for social recognition. Some students seek positive reinforcement from the teacher and the peer group, competing academically with classmates in order to be seen by them as doing well or poorly in school. Harris and Sipay (1980) discussing characteristics of remedial readers, note that many students feel that belonging to the peer group is a stronger need than is the desire to master reading skills. Some students actively resist accepting praise or acknowledgement for reading achievement because of desire to remain like other non-achieving members of the peer group. Individual progress charts which prevent cross-student comparisons can help improve poor readers' self-esteem without encouraging negative peer pressure for achievement. In other cases, positive reinforcement in front of the peer group motivates some students to continue to excell.

Need to avoid failure. Students wishing to avoid failure and who fear school failure often have such a high level of anxiety related to school performance that failure results. Anxiety reduction therapy, provided by a trained counselor, can often help children with high tension resulting from a desire to avoid failure to master their self-defeating behaviors. Biofeedback is sometimes a suggested treatment for such children, since this technique helps them internalize locus of control and develop an attitude of confidence and responsibility toward learning to read.

Desire to conform. Students work at academic tasks because it is "demanded by parents or teachers, or, if relevant, peers" (Chiu, 1967). Conformity helps ensure belongingness and love; meeting the expressed wishes of a teacher also helps conforming children raise self-esteem. The present educational

74

system usually rewards conformity in classroom behavior.

Students' perceptions, values, personalities, and judgements. If a student perceives reading as an important activity, and learns to value reading for enjoyment and problem solving, he is likely to be more motivated to learn to read. Individual's personalities and judgements also affect reading motivation. A personality that lends itself to on-task behavior usually results in higher achievement over time. Positive judgements about learning to read related to self-esteem and self-actualization are generally present in good readers.

In summary, the idea that teachers motivate students is a myth. Each person is responsible for his/her own motivation. Teachers should consider the factors which affect motivation, and then provide opportunities and incentives for reading, match reading interests with instructional activities, and structure the reading/learning environment so that learning is attractive and stimulating. But the students motivate themselves (Wlodkowski, 1978).

Factors Affecting Self-concept

Three factors affect children's self-concept as it relates to reading: parental behavior, self-esteem, and self-consistency.

Parental behavior. Children learn to perceive the attitudes of significant adults (parents and, at the primary grade levels, teachers) toward them, and come to accept these evaluations as true (Hanachek, 1971). If a young reader with poor oral reading fluency reads aloud to parents who expect perfection, and parents offer criticism, the child can accept the parents' evaluation that he/she is a poor reader. A "You're OK" atmosphere in the home helps children develop resiliency to failure, and an acceptance of self-worth.

Self-esteem. Self-esteem is defined as the wish to think well of one's self. It is the individual's sense of worth which is based partially on competence. A child who is a poor reader generally has a low self-esteem related to reading, because the child is aware that he/she is having difficulty.

Self-consistency. The motive to act in accordance

with the self-concept and to maintain it in the face of potentially-challenging evidence is termed self-consistency. The actual self may change, yet the self view may remain the same. Individual decisions are based not on what we are, but on what we think we are. A poor reader who becomes a better reader may still have a poor self-concept related to his/her reading ability, because he/she still believes he/she is a disabled reader.

Assessing Reading Motivation and Self-concept

Motivation and self-concept related to reading achievement are area specific; research shows that global measurement of these two hypothetical constructs is unlikely to provide reading educators with knowledge specific enough to be of assistance in planning effective instruction.

Several methods can be employed in the measurement of motivation and self-concept related to reading achievement. Each measure described below has sound theoretical and instructional foundations which add vitality to the measure:

1. Likert-like scales (1932) have been used to measure reading attitude, a factor affecting motivation. The best-known instrument (normed and validated) is the Estes Attitude Scales: Primary and Secondary which has two forms, one for elementary and a second for secondary students (Estes, Johnstone, and Richards, 1976). Students read statements and indicate whether they strongly agree, agree, are unsure, disagree or strongly disagree with the statements. The instrument provides a quantitative measure of attitude toward reading, which may be used in pre-posttesting of students.

   Mikulecky's Behavioral Attitude Measure (1976) uses the Very Like Me-Very Unlike Me scale to determine a student's response to observable reading behaviors, which are correlated with Krathwhol's levels of value development. This measure is appropriate for students in grade levels five and above.

2. The semantic differential (Osgood, Suci, and Tannenbaum, 1957) is a valid tool in the measurement of reading motivation and self-

76

concept. Teachers can compose statements about reading motivation and self-concept and ask students to respond to a set of seven point scales employing bipolar adjectives (good-bad, strong-weak). The students read the statement and indicate their reaction by marking the scale.

Example: Reading makes me feel good about myself.

Good___ ___ ___ ___ ___ ___ ___ ___Bad

Weak___ ___ ___ ___ ___ ___ ___ ___Strong

A quantitative measure, the semantic differential is a strong accurate way of assessing reading motivation and attitude.

3. Teacher observation of student behaviors (e.g., noting the number of books checked out of the school library in a month-long period, students' selection of reading as an activity during free time, etc.) can help teachers measure motivation and self-concept related to reading. Assessing students' interests through interest inventories (Harris and Sipay, 1980), direct observation of book choices, observation of attentiveness and resistance to distraction during free reading time are all methods of determining students' reading motivation and self-concept.

Increasing Reading Motivation and Self-concept

There are three learning processes by which a child's reading motivation and self-concept can be modified through learning. Realize, however, that as a child matures and develops autonomy, these processes become less effective. Classical conditioning, reinforcement, and imitation are all means by which teachers can help children develop good self-concept and appropriate levels of motivation as they strive to achieve in reading. Effective instruction capitalizes on all three processes at appropriate times in order to meet individual needs. A brief description of each learning process follows, accompanied by general and specific suggestions for increasing reading achievement through development of motivation and self-concept.

Classical Conditioning

Pavlovian stimulus-response conditioning led to behaviorism a la John Watson, who formulated the principle of feeling tone. The association of pleasant feeling tone with reading will increase reading motivation and self-concept to a high degree. Unpleasant feeling tone will also increase motivation, but to a lesser degree (and there may be undesirable side effects) (Hunter, 1967). Neutral or absence of feeling tone will not affect children's motivation. Feeling tone related to reading should include: developing positive expectations on the part of the teacher (the corollary is that instruction must be provided on the instructional level), encouraging students' perceptions of success, and maximizing individual achievement (Schuman and Fox, 1980). Cashin (1979) provides a collection of suggestions for improving feeling tone related to student motivation, grouped under the following headings: Begin where the students are, establish the relevance of the course material, and involve the students in the choice of what will be studied. He suggests that motivation is a significant variable in students' readiness and willingness to learn to read, that students are innately curious and do want to know and understand, that provision for successful accomplishments at a fairly consistent rate is motivating, and that teachers can create an atmosphere where learning will be more efficient.

Classrooms with relaxed atmospheres, which allow children a degree of freedom to explore the world, encourage curiosity and decrease anxiety. The optimal time for development of curiosity is during preschool and the early primary years. While academic environments should be structured, they should be neither boring nor too unfamiliar, because discomfort, restlessness, and aversion may result (Vidler, 1977). Such behaviors are indicative of negative feeling tone, which remains linked to whatever learning occurs.

The physical setting in a classroom can be structured to create positive feeling tone. Create a reading corner in your classroom which provides children with a quiet place to read for pleasure in books they have selected. Companies that deal in floor coverings are generous in donating carpet squares which can be used to form a patchwork carpet. Or, if you enjoy prowling in junk stores, keep on the lookout for an old-fashioned bathtub with four legs. Fill it with pillows instead of water, and watch the children in

78

your classroom bathe themselves in books. Ask parents to help their children make personalized reading pillows for the recreational reading corner. Such materials add to a warm, comfortable classroom environment conducive to developing motivation in reading (Book bonanza, 1980).

Teachers can help structure classrooms with relaxed atmospheres which meet the students' need for limits and regulation, and for freedom, and self-expression, by following these guidelines:

1. Begin where the students are.

Employ a diagnostic-prescriptive methodology for teaching reading skills, and share the results of the diagnosis with the student, asking for his/her input as you plan the prescriptive program. Be sure to word results in terms the student can understand.

Establish realistic goals based on a reader's strengths and weaknesses, determine a concrete plan of action, and measure progress and effort related to mastery of reading skills. Reduce praise and increase encouragement. Emphasize the process of learning, not the completed product. As students work toward mastery, emphasize accomplishments and point out incorrect responses, providing suggestions for improvement in a positive way.

Guarantee successful learning by teaching the student on his/her instructional level, while emphasizing the student's responsibility in the learning process. Instructional materials should be geared to students' level of ability, so that children are usually successful in mastering them. Competition should be discouraged when it constantly leads to failure for a particular child or group of children (Hansen, 1977).

Recognize the difficulty involved in learning and convey a realistic expectancy toward learning to the student. Never imply that the task is simple or easy. If a student succeeds--the task was too easy in the first place. If he fails, he has a deeper sense of failure because he failed a simplistic task. Help students write contracts as a means of

realistic goal setting. Be sure to include a
time line, and provisions for illness or other
interferences. If necessary, segment the
learning task by dividing it into manageable
components. A student may try to learn 10
basic sight words when he could balk at
attempting to pronounce the 220 Dolch words
at one sitting.

2. <u>Establish</u> the <u>relevance</u> of the <u>course</u>
<u>material</u>.

Page and Pinnell (1979) suggest that one
key factor in reading comprehension and motivation is the reader's own purpose for reading
the story, poem, or play. How can teachers
examine this factor with their own students?
Page and Pinnell suggest that the teacher
lead a class discussion of the following
questions: 1) Why do people read? 2) What did
you read last week? 3) What's so important
about reading? 4) Why do you want to learn to
read better? 5) What do you have to do to
learn to read? 6) How can you tell you're a
good teacher? 7) How can you tell you're not
a good reader? The classroom teacher may
discover some misconceptions on the part of
her students which may help her understand
why some of her students have poor attitudes
and self-concepts about reading. The authors
suggest ways to help students develop the
concept of meaningful reading, based on
students establishing their own purpose for
reading.

Psychological research (Morris and Melvin,
1981) lends considerable support to the view
that a positive self-concept is likely to
result in high achievement levels; the same
field of research further indicates that a
negative self-concept is likely to be
associated with underachievement and failure.
Numerous research efforts have concluded that
attitudes, beliefs, and feelings associated
with self-concept have significant influence
on how closely a person approaches his learning potential. When students were asked
questions related to school learning and
Maslow's hierarchy of needs, most students
felt that if their needs were met, motivation
might increase. Reading for information in

80

order to meet needs perceived by the students would make reading more meaningful to many students.

Heller and Hornby (1981), who studied sixth grade students who had previously experienced reading failure and had been labeled as handicapped, found these students were disruptive and exhibited reading avoidance behavior. The investigators replaced the medical model (diagnosing and "curing" the reading deficit) with a model focusing on providing students with 1) a need to seek information by reading and 2) encouragement for work done. Students' self-concepts improved as they worked on small-group and whole class assignments rather than individually on specific skill worksheets. Behavioral changes attributed to this approach included reduced reading avoidance behavior and increased interest in recreational reading. The authors include guidelines for employment of this approach in the classroom, which focuses on reading for meaningful problem solving.

Classroom teachers who are trying to help students develop motivation in reading might try these activities: Read menus from students' favorite restaurants (you'll be surprised at interest of the students, which may be related to hunger!). Write shapebooks during your language experience lesson, since the shapes stimulate students' thinking and subsequent composition/reading activities. Suggested shapes include the body of a child (possible title: All About ME), TV set (My TV Favorites); baseball or football or tennis racquet (My Sports Heroes); airplane (Travel); schoolhouse (School Events). These activities appeal to the egocentricity of the students, and are therefore motivating and meaningful.

Students can practice their reading and writing skills in a meaningful context as they write to postmasters in certain towns with fascinating names, inquiring as to the historical significance of the name of the town (Cook and Swanson, 1979). In this activity reading is used as a tool for dis-

81

covery, in order to satisfy curiosity, and
becomes more relevant to many children.

Crime literature can be employed as a
motivational tool for teaching reading and
English (Kerschgens, 1978). One teacher's
stint on jury duty (Shawn, 1978) led her to
place literature on trial in her classroom.
Self-directed dramatizations involved students
acting as the accused, the judge, members of
the jury, witnesses, and prosecuting and
defense attorneys. A selected short story,
with an ambiguous ending, was the focus for a
jury trial for a suspected murder. Students
actively participated in the trial and demonstrated a much higher level of inferential
and evaluative reading comprehension.

A unit on motorcycles helped remedial
reading students experience meaningful reading, as they read a book on motorcycles; made
a comparative chart on the costs of different
motorcycles, their maintenance, and size; and
wrote motorcycle companies about their prod-
ucts. The state driver's manual provided
reading comprehension exercises, while an
interview with a state police officer resulted
in composition of mock newspaper articles. An
imaginary cross-country trip, focusing on
research skills and mapreading, was the final
activity, which ended a meaningful unit based
on students' interests and needs (Interchange,
1980).

3. Involve the children in the choice of what
   will be studied.

Ley (1979) suggests that individualized
reading can be employed to personalize the
literature/reading program in the secondary
school. Students allowed to choose their own
books, read along with taped stories, visit
the library and read at their own pace will
develop better self-concepts and become more
motivated. Teacher-student interaction during
scheduled book conferences allows teachers to
model on a one-on-one basis their own love
and appreciation for reading, while meaningful
questions related to students' comments about
the books assists in the development of reading comprehension at higher levels.

Gentile and McMillan (1979) emphasize the need for adolescents to discover their own reading interests and needs; the classroom teacher then suggests reading materials which match these interests and needs and are on the correct level of difficulty. Activities focusing on instructional increments which allow frequent success, immediate feedback specific to students' responses, and self-selection of books based on interests are presented in the handbook Methods for Motivation, Grades 7-9 (1981).

Paperbacks at hand in the classroom and in the school library lure students to recreational reading. Sharp (1981) provides a suggested booklist of popular children's paperbacks, while Browder (1981) the proprietor of a children's bookshop, describes the unique characteristics paperbacks possess for motivating children's interest in recreational reading. Incidently, children's interest in the material they are reading often helps them combat the high readability level of the book or magazine. (In addition to paperbacks, Strelecki (1979) suggests teachers make popular magazines a part of the reading program.)

Where can students obtain paperback books of high interest to them? Perhaps the best known motivational device for encouraging more reading through student's self-selection and ownership of books is the book club. Scholastic Book Services, the Read Book Club (sponsored by Xerox Educational Publications), and the Troll Book Club (Troll Associates) offer students a choice of approximately 30 titles monthly. Book fairs, usually organized on a schoolwide basis, with paperback books donated by students, offer students inexpensive books which can stimulate wide reading. Profits are used to purchase additional books for the next fair. Both the book fair and book clubs need some preliminary publicity and promotion. School announcements, teacher talks, posters, and book previews are effective ways to increase students' interests (Conors and Gray, 1979). Field (1979) mentions a book exchange program where teachers and students brought books and magazines to school, and then exchanged them.

Self-selection of books, and the opportunity to own books, may help young readers to begin to appreciate reading as an enjoyable activity (Zibart, 1980). RIF (Reading Is Fundamental) has distributed millions of free paperback books in a school reading-motivation program.

Another inexpensive, highly-motivating way of providing students with inexpensive reading materials is to establish a school publishing company. A school publishing company can provide concrete evidence of students' creativity and composition skills, as well as motivation for reading (How many of these bestsellers have you read?, 1981).

Calloway's (1981) study of some 200 college students revealed that students felt paperback book clubs and teachers who make reading enjoyable left lasting positive impressions on these students, while oral reading and dull materials were factors students felt discouraged reading.

A teacher of the deaf capitalized upon children's innate egocentricity and wrote stories featuring his students in situations showing them to be brave, strong, and good. Another story character asked the student mentioned in the story to answer higher level questions in order for the study to be completed (Mothner, 1980). The children helped determine the story ending.

Koenke (1978), summarizing research in the area of motivation and reading, incorporates suggestions for several studies for the classroom teacher concerned about motivating students in reading. Language experience and individualized reading instruction, as described by Allen and Veatch, are intrinsic motivators, whereas phonics and single skill instruction are not. Folklore, its collection and transcribing, can provide educational material that meets students' needs in several ways: emphasizing the pride of different ethnic groups, meaningful use of reading and

84

writing, and student input in what is studied. A Foxfire publication, presenting folklore and dialect materials, can preserve stories and skills unique to particular individuals and communities.

Activities involving arts and crafts can spark reading interest in unmotivated readers (Jansson and Schillereff, 1980). Puppets can be used as motivational devices for children of all ages. The students read about how to make the puppets, write or rewrite a script, and then work with the script and finished puppets to complete a finished puppet show for presentation to parents and other children (Rivers, 1979; Ramsey, 1979). Monsters fascinate primary-age children, and Lee Hopkins (1980) capitalizes on that interest in a reading program centered around monsters. Books, films, multimedia programs, and other resources to help teachers prepare for the same type of program are described in an article which appeared in Teacher. Children can choose to illustrate monster stories, make monster costumes, and read monster books, a wide selection of which are provided on different levels.

Capitalize upon humor as a motivational and remedial technique (Colwell, 1981). The thrill of reading and the fun can be recaptured by requesting that students read jokes and humorous material aloud (after some practice with a peer or the classroom teacher) (Open to suggestion, 1981). Klasky (1979) shares suggestions for employing humorous stories and comedy routines in individual oral reading and comprehension activities and for group skits. A preliminary readability study of 20 popular comic strips provides evidence that many comics are easy reading materials which have the added motivational devices of art, humor, and similar interests to encourage the reluctant reader (Wright, 1979). Students' self-selection of humorous materials to read and share is important, since self-selection meets individuals' needs to help determine what they will be reading and learning.

Reinforcement

Edward Thorndike's Law of Effect states: When a modifiable connection between a stimulus and response is made, and the condition is followed by a satisfying state of affairs, the connection is strengthened (Thorndike, 1913). Positive reinforcement following reading helps build intrinsic motivation in the student to read again.

The age and background of the student affect the application and strength of the reinforcement. Poor readers need small, immediate rewards rather than larger, delayed rewards. An A on a child's report card at the end of a six-week period is an ineffective reinforcer for the student's efforts. Since not all reinforcers work for all children with the same degree of success, the classroom teacher must determine which reinforcements are appropriate for individual children at given periods of time (remember: preferences change!).

The most potent values of reinforcement are 1) to develop self-sustaining motivational habits in the reader, and 2) to build self-concept based on students' knowledge of reading competency. Remember to reinforce and recognize effort as well as accomplishments. Reward the student who is willing to try, saying often, "I like the way you try!"

Provide consistent immediate feedback regarding mastery of learning through:

1. Peer tutoring. Tutors should be trained to immediately tell the remedial reader whether he was correct in his response, and if not, to explain the correct response. In an experiment conducted by Rodick and Henggeler (1980), results show statistically-significant gains in reading achievement for students tutored by non-professional tutors, when students were required to set realistic goals, and reinforcement was social interaction for successful completion of stated goals.

2. Self-checking. Provide the students with keys to the assigned exercises, and let them check their own work and correct their errors. If you fear a student will simply copy the correct answers from the answer key, keep the

86

answer key at your desk until the student has shown you he has completed the assignment.

Pair low-interest activities with high-interest activities whenever possible. For instance, pair skill instruction in sequencing and reading to follow directions with building a model or a kite or sewing a dress or cooking. Use interest inventories to determine students' interests and then stock the classroom with appropriate activities and reading materials.

Field trips and other community exploration activities can show students that reading exists as a meaningful skill outside the classroom (Fredericks, 1980). (Be sure to check school and individual insurance policies before leaving the school grounds.) Language experience stories about the field trip can then be used for skill development.

Gough (1979) notes that instructional television using special programming can motivate student readers. Once students have watched the TV program, they may enjoy reading the original script of the show. In one Louisiana high school students watching the movie "Reds" became curious about the historical accuracy of the lives of the people portrayed in the movie and spent time in the school library researching the lives of the characters and the historical events protrayed, including the Depression, formation of labor unions, the American Communist Party, the Bolshevik Revolution, and Eugene O'Neil's plays.

Display students' work prominently in the classroom and change the displays frequently. For example, a spirit medicine bottle (Rx for low spirits to be taken as needed with daily practice) was employed by a classroom teacher who asked students to collect items from books, magazines, or newspapers which made them feel better (raised their spirits). Humor and comedy were evidenced as students shaped covers of their home-made books into prescription bottles, and cut pages to match the shape of the cover. Book format was also studied using this same shape book (Interchange, 1981, 81). Shape books were displayed within the classroom and shared with other students.

Free reading time in books of their choice is a reinforcer that helps students build motivation. Appealing to students' fascination with comic books, one librarian added Spiderman and his cronies to her library. Library circulation of noncomic materials increased by 30 percent, and overall library usage by 82 percent, with only minimal comic collection security problems at one junior high school in Missouri (Dorrell and Carroll, 1981).

Free reading is successful when children have immediate access to books, or books are provided directly to the children. To combat summer learning loss among remedial readers, teachers and consultants in the Omaha, Nebraska, Title I program designed a set of comic-book reading units and mailed them to the children's homes during the summer. Parents were pleased with the program, which helped students maintain reading gains from the previous school year (Meyer and Buckner, 1980). Another method of providing access to books and helping to decrease loss of reading achievement over the summer vacation is to allow students who have a history of regular use of the school library to check out ten books of their choice during the last week of school. Place the books in a sturdy plastic bag for easy carrying. Don't require book reports, check tests, or parental signatures as a means of checking on the students' reading. At the end of the summer, students return their books to the school library (Conors and Gray, 1979).

Reinforcement for reading should emphasize concrete record keeping of students' progress in reading, which is one means of providing immediate feedback. To reinforce students' sense of achievement after free reading periods, Conors and Gray (1979) suggest two plans of action: 1) a bookworm that grows as students add body segments bearing students' names and the books read; and 2) a "Reading Wall of Fame" where students' photographs are placed after they have read a certain number of books. Both ideas benefit from school-wide participation, which will increase students' motivation and participation in free reading activities.

Support, on a school-wide basis, activities to reinforce children's reading; 1) Design a bookmark contest, where the winner at each grade level is awarded a T-shirt with his bookmark printed on it, and the winning bookmarks are printed and distributed to children who have read at least one book during the last six weeks. Parents and administrators would serve as judges; 2) Advertise books, billboard style, on the walls of the school. Award a prize to the designer of the best billboard; 3) Paperback book drives are one way of obtaining additional materials for the school

and classroom library. Award a prize to the classroom
collecting the largest number of books (Book bonanza,
1980).

Imitation

Children learn by imitating or modeling the behavior of their peers and significant adults. (Did
you know that aggressive teachers tend to have
aggressive students?) If reading teachers want their
students to develop curiosity and the habit of inquiring, they should model curiosity and inquiry. If
reading teachers want children to develop life-long
reading habits, they should model life-long reading
habits. Classroom teachers, administrators, librarians,
and parents are significant adults whom children
imitate. Children who observe these adults reading,
and valuing reading, become readers themselves. How
can these adults model reading behavior? Read on;
examples follow.

1. Classroom teachers

Teachers who love to read, and show their enjoyment to their students, can affect their classes'
motivation (Chantland, 1979).

Model enthusiasm for reading. Read aloud to
students regularly and project your enjoyment. Let
students see you reading and enjoying what you read.
Associate the student who dislikes reading with peers
who are enthusiastic readers. Let these children
share books, stories, poems, and their own language
experience stories.

Provide school time for structured recreational
reading; One way of encouraging unmotivated students
to read on a regular basis is to provide materials of
interest to them. Galen and Prendergast (1979)
describe the uninterrupted sustained silent reading
method which capitalizes on the teacher as a model for
recreational reading.

Letters from authors of children's books can act
as a major motivational technique to involve students
(Lee, 1979). Children learn that a real person
resides behind the concept "author."

When adolescents are asked to write about personal
experiences, problems, and dilemmas they have faced, in
a form of language experience, they frequently show

interest in sharing their stories with one another, and in reading each others' writings (McWilliams and Smith, 1981). Poor readers learn from sharing with and imitating good readers.

Encouraging students to discuss controversial issues in relation to their reading can help improve comprehension and can also motivate students by capitalizing on their enjoyment of class discussion and their identification with the characters in the materials under discussion (Lunstrum, 1981).

Self-directed dramatization (activities in which children direct themselves as they act out characters in stories they have read) can help students determine their own attitudes and interests (Vawter and Vancil, 1980). Such dramatizations can also help improve self-concept and motivation related to reading, since the dramatization occurs as a result of the reading, and reinforces such skills as oral reading fluency and comprehension as it is reflected in oral interpretation of characters' moods and personalities.

Discussions of controversial topics and self-directed dramatizations can lead teachers to direct individual students to specific books related to a student's problems or needs, one form of bibliotherapy, wherein a student reads a story or novel and vicariously imitates a character in order to learn a lesson or discover a truth.

Bibliotherapy is the attempt to promote mental and emotional health by using reading materials to meet individual needs, reduce anxiety, or assist in personal development. Theoretically, the reader identifies with the story character and catharsis occurs through the vicarious reading experience (Harris and Sipay, 1980). Insight follows and the reader's anxieties are relieved.

Schrank and Engels (1981) suggest bibliotherapy as an adjunct to counseling students. The classroom teacher, school librarian and counselor work as a team, with the classroom teacher providing the students' instructional levels and his/her perception of the problem, the librarian suggesting well-written books on that instructional level in which authors portray similar-aged children with similar problems, and the counselor meeting with the student regularly to talk about the student's reaction to the book in terms of his/her own problem.

90

Guthrie (1979) summarizes research designed to measure reader's identification with major story characters. The basis for identification is the similarity of the emotional state of the reader and the feelings portrayed by a character in the story. Such evidence strongly supports the use of bibliotherapy by trained counselors as a means of helping students with adjustment problems resulting from divorce of parents, death, drug abuse, etc. Mangieri, Bader, and Walker (1982) provide a detailed listing of suggested book titles for bibliotherapy, including author and illustrator, title, publisher, suggested grade level for use of the title, and theme of the book.

2. Administrators

Principals, assistant principals, and guidance counselors are significant others to most school children, many of whom look to these administrators as examples for imitation. Administrators who demonstrate personal enjoyment of reading, and who show students the high priority and value they attach to the school reading program, are likely to help students develop positive motivation and self-concept related to reading. As a result, students' reading achievement will increase.

One principal in a rural elementary school in southwestern Louisiana started a principal's reading club, the "Gator Club." An artist, he drew alligators on tagboard, and provided six spaces along the back of the alligator for children to write in six titles of books they had read during a six-week period. Any child who read six books in six weeks and briefly summarized the books during an oral discussion with the principal, became a member in good standing in the "Gator Club" and received a hand-drawn alligator progress chart. In order to remain in goodstanding, students have to continue to read regularly.

Another principal reads aloud regularly to children, moving from classroom to classroom, sharing excerpts from books which tempt children to check the books out of the school library and read them for themselves.

An administrator who values reading, and places a high priority on reading achievement, may be the single most influential factor in developing a successful school reading program.

3. Librarians

The school librarian is the heart of the school reading program--she has the books!

One objective frequently cited by librarians is the development and promotion of reading as a life-long learning and recreational habit (Librarians and English teachers: Part II, 1981). Suggestions for increasing the lines of communication between English teachers and school librarians are offered in this article from the English Journal. The school librarian is often able to assist the classroom teacher in reaching the able but unwilling reader (Rabban, 1980). The librarian can provide a variety of reading materials and assist in encouraging reading both during the library period and in the classroom.

Librarians can organize book fairs, go from classroom to classroom "sharing" excerpts from new books, and match readers' interests to specific titles. Classroom teachers should provide librarians with students' independent reading levels and reading interests so that the librarian can provide better "fit" between the child and the book.

4. Parents

Schubert (1978) feels that both the home and the school can help develop self-concept resulting in reading improvement. He suggests that parents should show respect and love for their children, set realistic standards and expectations, praise effort as well as achievement, resist the temptation to compare siblings, establish consistent discipline procedures, and be hesitant about teaching their own children to read. Teachers should provide a warm supportive atmosphere for reading instruction, cultivate humor in the classroom, hold high expectations for achievement, foster individuality, and provide students with a multitude of opportunities for success in work on their own level of achievement.

As teachers, we want to teach students to become independent learners, so that they can come to accept some of the responsibility for learning. Encourage parents to assign chores to students at home which must be completed on a regular basis (water the dog, take out the garbage, feed the goldfish, clear the table, etc.). Responsibility in the home will carry-over to responsibility at school. Criscuolo (1980) and

92

Schubert (1978) suggest effective ways that parents and teachers can work together to motivate children to read and enhance children's self-images.

Parent-child interaction through a "Personalized Contract Book Program" can help provide a nonpressured environment in the home that will help foster students' reading (Cholewinski and Holliday, 1979). Children model and imitate significant others, and the most significant others at the kindergarten and primary grade levels are their parents.

Unfortunately, reading is generally viewed by Americans as a feminine activity. In order to provide first grade students with models of adult male readers, one teacher sent home messages urging fathers to read aloud to their children regularly (Interchange, 1981, 579). Some fathers came to the classroom to share their profession or hobbies with the children, read books aloud, or share recreational reading time. In another program, community members joined in a "read-in" and read to children in small groups and classrooms in a project designed to improve students' self-concepts (Interchange, 1979).

Children imitate and become what they see, and if what they see are significant adults (parents, teachers, administrators, and librarians) enjoying reading and learning from reading, they are more likely to develop lifelong reading habits, which is the stated goal of reading teachers.

Summary

Practitioners who request inservice programs dealing with motivation and/or self-concept as they relate to reading achievement are supported by the literature, which does suggest that motivation and self-concept specific to the act of reading can affect reading ability and achievement. Teachers who are aware of the factors affecting motivation and self-concept related to reading achievement can plan instruction designed to capitalize on these factors and increase students' motivation and self-concept. Once a teacher has assessed students in these two affective areas, he/she should be able to employ classical conditioning, reinforcement, and/or imitation in designing both an educational environment and specific instruction which will increase reading achievement.

Reference Notes

1. Chiu, L. H. A factoral study of academic motivation. Unpublished doctoral dissertation,
   Teachers College, Columbia University, 1967.

2. Mikulecky, L. J. The developing, field-testing,
   and initial norming of a secondary/adult
   reading attitude measure that is behaviorally-
   oriented and based on Krathwohl's Taxonomy of
   the Affective Domain. Unpublished doctoral
   dissertation, University of Wisconsin, Madison,
   1976.

References

Ball, S. Introduction. In S. Ball (Ed.), Motivation
   in education. New York: Academic Press, 1977.

Book bonanza. Instructor, 1980, 90, 44-51.

Browder, R. The password is paperbacks. Horn Book
   Magazine, 1981, 57, 30-37.

Butkowsky, I. S., & Willows, D. M. Cognitive-
   motivational characteristics of children varying
   in reading ability: Evidence for learned help-
   lessness in poor readers. Journal of Educational
   Psychology, 1980, 72, 408-422.

Calloway, B. What turns children "on" or "off" in
   reading. Reading Improvement, 1981, 18, 214-217.

Cashin, W. E. Motivating students. IDEA paper no. 1.
   Manhattan, Kansas: Kansas State University
   Center for Faculty Evaluation and Development in
   Higher Education, 1979. (ERIC Document Reproduc-
   tion Service No. ED 202 409)

Chantland, G. C. Teaching is loving something so much
   that your students learn to love it, too. Today's
   Education, 1979, 68, 73, 68.

Cholewinski, M. E., Holliday, S. Learning to read:
   What's right at home is right at school. Language
   Arts, 1979, 56, 671-674.

Colwell, C. G. Humor as a motivational and remedial
   technique. Journal of Reading, 1981, 24, 484-486.

Conors, P. M. & Gray, R. H. Selling books: Literally and figuratively. English Journal, 1979, 68, 37-39.

Cook, J. E., & Swanson, D. M. Uneeda Helper Ina Reading Center? Journal of Reading, 1979, 22, 531-533.

Cramer, E. H., & Schubert, W. H. Reading Skills management systems--Do they really work? Curriculum Review, 1979, 18, 392-395.

Criscuolo, N. P. Reading motivation through the teacher-parent partnership. Momentum, 1980, 11, 21-23.

Doggett, M. Aiding the moderately deficient readers at the secondary level. Kappa Delta Pi Record, 1979, 16, 54-57.

Dorrell, L., & Carroll, E. Spider Man at the library. School Library Journal, 1981, 27, 17-19.

Estes, T., Johnstone, J. P., & Richards, H. C. Estes Attitude Scales: Manual for Administration and Interpretation. Charlottesville, VA: Virginia Research Associates, 1976.

Field, J. T. Classroom tips. Today's Education, 1979, 68, 82-83.

Fredericks, A. D. Get reading out of your classroom. Instructor, 1980, 90, 150, 152.

Galen, N., & Prendergast, J. Selling Reading. Reading Horizons, 1979, 19, 280-283.

Gentile, L. M., & McMillan, M. Making reading real: Books and self-awareness. Journal of Reading, 1979, 22, 629-633.

Goodacre, E. Reading research in Great Britain - 1979. Reading, 1980, 14, 3-11.

Gose, A., Wooden, S., & Muller, D. The relative potential of self-concept and intelligence as predictors of achievement. The Journal of Psychology, 1980, 104, 279-287.

Gough, P. B. Introducing children to books via television. Reading Teacher, 1979, 32, 458-462.

Guthrie, J. T. Research views: To want to read. Reading Teacher, 1979, 32, 990-992.

Hanachek, D. E. Encounters with the self. New York: Holt, 1971.

Hansen, R. A. Anxiety. In S. Ball (Ed.), Motivation in education. New York: Academic Press, 1977.

Harris, A. J. & Sipay, E. R. How to increase reading ability: A guide to developmental and remedial methods. Seventh edition. New York: Longman, Inc., 1980.

Heller, M., & Hornby, J. Is the medical model making our children sick--of reading? Paper presented at the annual meeting of the Plains Regional Conference of the International Reading Association, Des Moines, Iowa, October 22-24, 1981. (ERIC Document Reproduction Service No. ED 208 385)

Hopkins, L. B. Book bonanza: The chill factor: Monsters we know and love. Teacher, 1980, 97, 32, 34, 36, 38.

How many of these bestsellers have you read? Instructor, 1981, 91, 72-73.

Hunter, M. Motivation Theory for Teachers: A Programmed Book. El Segundo, CA: TIP Publications, 1967.

Interchange. Reading Teacher, 1979, 33, 344-346.

Interchange. Reading Teacher, 1980, 33, 830-835.

Interchange. Reading Teacher, 1981, 34, 576-579.

Interchange. Reading Teacher, 1981, 35, 80-84.

Jansson, D. R., & Schillereff, T. A. Reinforcing remedial readers through art activities. Reading Teacher, 1980, 33, 548-551.

Kerschgens, E. "Who killed Baker?" A crime story in the Hauptschule. Englisch, 1978, 13, 50-54.

96

Klasky, C. Some funny business in your reading class. *Journal* *of* *Reading*, 1979, <u>22</u>, 731-733.

Koenke, K. Motivation and reading: ERIC/RCS report. *Language* *Arts*, 1978, <u>55</u>, 998-1002.

Krech, D., Crutchfield, R. S., & Ballochey, E. L. *Individuals* *in* *society*: A *textbook* *of* *social* *psychology*. New York: McGraw-Hill, 1962.

Lee, J. W. Messages from Matthew: An unexpected resource. *Language* *Arts*, 1979, <u>56</u>, 278-280.

Lehn, T. The short-term predictive validity of a standardized reading test and of scales reflecting six dimensions of academic self-concept relative to selected high school achievement criteria for four ethnic groups. *Educational* *and* *Psychological* *Measurement*, 1980, <u>40</u>, 1017-1031.

Ley, T. C. Getting kids into books: The importance of individualized reading. *Media* *and* *Methods*, 1979, <u>15</u>, 22-24.

Librarians and English teachers: Part II. *English* *Journal*, 1981, <u>70</u>, 75-77.

Likert, R. A technique for the measurement of attitude. *Archives* *of* *psychology*, 1932, <u>22</u>, 140.

Lunstrum, J. P. Building motivation through the use of controversy. *Journal* *of* *Reading*, 1981, <u>24</u>, 687-691.

McWilliams, L., & Smith, D. L. Decision stories: Language experience for adolescents. *Journal* *of* *Reading*, 1981, <u>25</u>, 142-145.

Mangieri, J. N., Bader, L. A., & Walker, J. A. *Elementary* *reading*: A *comprehensive* *approach*. New York: McGraw-Hill, 1982.

Maslow, A. H. *Towards* *a* *psychology* *of* *being*. New York: D. Van Nostrand and Co., 1968.

Methods *for* *Motivation*, *Grades* *7-9*. Indianapolis, Indiana: Indiana State Department of Public Instruction, Division of Reading Effectiveness, 1981. (ERIC Document Reproduction Service No. ED 210 647)

Meyer, R., & Buckner, J. Superheroes and summer reading. Instructor, 1980, 89, 83.

Morris, R. C., & Melvin, E. A. An assessment of
student perceptions of needs and deficiencies.
Education, 1981, 102, 2-12.

Mothner, H. A technique for teaching the unmotivated
reading. American Annals of the Deaf, 1980, 125,
551-553.

Neufeld, J. S., & Cozac, E. A study of the self-
concept of intellectually superior children.
Alberta Journal of Educational Research, 1980,
26, 149-148.

Open to suggestion. Journal of Reading, 1981, 25,
272-276.

Osgood, C. E., Suci, G. J., & Tannenbaum, P. H. The
measurement of meaning. Urbana: The University
of Illinois Press, 1957.

Page, W. D., & Pinnell, G. S. Developing purposes for
reading. Today's Education, 1979, 68, 52-55.

Rabban, E. Reaching the able but unwilling reader.
School Library Journal, 1980, 27, 37.

Ramsey, I. L. Puppetry. Audiovisual Instruction,
1979, 24, 28-29.

Rivers, S. N. Puppets with a purpose. Reading Teacher,
1979, 32, 956-958.

Rodick, J. D., & Henggeler, S. W. The short-term and
long-term amelioration of academic and motivational deficiencies among low-achieving inner-city
adolescents. Child Development, 1980, 51, 1126-
1132.

Rosenberg, M. Conceiving the self. New York: Basic
Books, Inc., 1977.

Rust, L. W. Interests. In S. Ball (Ed.), Motivation
in education. New York: Academic Press, 1977.

Schrank, F. A., & Engels, D. W. Bibliotherapy as a
counseling adjunct: Research findings. Personnel
and Guidance Journal, 1981, 60, 143-147.

Schubert, D. G. Reading improvement through self-concept development. Reading Improvement, 1978, 15, 157-160.

Schuman, R. B., & Fox, Barbara. Professional concerns: remedial programs: Some strategies for creating a supportive learning environment. Reading Horizons, 1980, 20, 147-149.

Sharp, W. The paperback job. Horn Book Magazine, 1981, 57, 91-117.

Shawn, K. Literature on trial. In G. Stanford (Ed.), Activating the passive student: Classroom practices in teaching English, 1978-1979. Urbana: National Council of Teachers of English, 1978.

Shoemaker, A. L. Construct validity of area specific self-esteem: The Hare Self-Esteem Scale. Educational and Psychological Measurement, 1980, 40, 495-501.

Strelecki, K. Viewpoint: How did you know I was reading? English Journal, 1979, 68, 13-14.

Thorndike, E. L. An introduction to the theory of mental and social measurements. New York: Teachers College, Columbia University, 1913.

Torrence, E. P. Non-test ways of identifying the creatively gifted. In J. C. Gowan, G. D. Demos, & E. P. Torrence (Eds.), Creativity: Its educational implications. New York: Wiley, 1967.

Vawter, J. M., & Vancil, M. Helping children discover reading through self-directed dramatization. Reading Teacher, 1980, 34, 320-323.

Vidler, D. Curiosity. In S. Ball (Ed.), Motivation in education. New York: Academic Press, 1977.

Whaley, W. J. Self-esteem parents of child rearing and gain in reading achievement of disabled readers. Reading Improvement, 1979, 16, 242-247.

Wheeler, L., & Reilly, T. F. Self-concept and its relationship to academic achievement for EMR adolescents. Journal for Special Educators, 1980, 17, 78-83.

Wlodkowski, R. Motivation and teaching: A practical guide. Washington, D. C.: National Association of Education, 1978.

Wright, G. The comic strip in the classroom for the reluctant disabled reader. Reading Improvement, 1979, 16, 13-17.

Yarborough, B. H., & Johnson, R. A. A six-year study of sex differences in intellectual functioning, reading/language arts achievement, and affective development. Journal of Psychology, 1980, 106, 55-61.

Zibart, R. Children can love reading. Catholic Library World, 1980, 52, 113-114.

CHAPTER FOUR

READINESS ASSESSMENT AND DEVELOPMENT

PATRICIA A. EDWARDS
LOUISIANA TECH UNIVERSITY

Controversy as to when children are ready to read
has stirred debate for more than fifty years. According to Durkin (1970), to understand how "reading
readiness" got into professional vocabularies and then
into the school curriculum, it is necessary to go back
to the 1920's. The 1920's were marked by the beginning
of the so-called "scientific" measurement of human
behavior. The craze to measure literally everything
was characterized by the widespread use of school
surveys. Findings from these surveys revealed that
large numbers of children were failing first grade,
most often because of poor reading achievement.

Durkin (1970) correctly puts it when she says
researchers during the 1920's in their study of reading problems should have looked to such multiple and
commonsense causes as overly large classes, inappropri-
ate materials, inadequate teacher preparation, and
lack of motivation on the part of the children (p.
528). Instead these researchers readily assumed that
first graders were having difficulty learning to read
because they were not ready when the instructor started.
As a result, delaying reading instruction was recommended as the solution. Proponents of delayed
instruction in reading called it an "unnatural process"
and advocated postponement until the child reached the
age of eight. (Dewey, 1896; Huey, 1908). Research
data that attempted to pinpoint a specific mental age
for children to begin reading instruction was readily
adhered to by educators during the 1920's.

Researchers like Arthur (1925, Morphett and
Washburn, 1931) maintained that children were ready to
receive reading instruction when they reached the
mental age of six-and-one-half (6.5) years.

Mental age is computed in the following manner:
chronological age x (IQ/100) = mental age. Therefore,
if a child had just celebrated his or her sixth birth-
day and his or her IQ measured 110, the child's mental
age was calculated as 6.6 years - 6.0 x (110/100) -
and was said to be ready for reading instruction.
However, if a child with an IQ of 100 had just turned
six, then his or her mental age - 6 x 100/100 = 6.0

101

would be below the required 6.5 and reading instruction would be withheld.

Mental age is still being used today by some educators as an indicator of reading readiness (Fowler, 1971). But research conducted during the 1960's and 1970's tended to discredit complete reliance upon the mental age concept. Olson and Dillner (1982) summarize well six trends that tended to discredit the mental age concept.

1. Inadequacies of intelligence tests. Educators during the 1960's recognized that intelligence test results did not necessarily indicate a child's intelligence. The IQ tests were found to be culturally biased, giving accurate results for white, middle-class children only.

2. Positive response to preschool education of children with mental age of less than 6.5. Research data during the 1960's indicated that those children who had received training in the skills prerequisite to reading (reading readiness skills) were ready for formal reading instruction at an earlier age than were children who had received no such instruction.

3. Introduction of formal reading instruction in the preschool. Many preschools are now offering reading instruction as part of the curriculum, and many children with mental ages of less than 6.5 appear to be profiting from such instruction.

4. Assessing and teaching cognitive skills. Piaget's theories have recently begun to be related to reading instruction. Piaget's greatest contribution appears to be his theory that children must understand certain concepts, such as conservation, before they are able to profit from reading instruction (Kirkland, 1978). Research indicates that concepts such as conservation should be developed before reading instruction begins, and researchers believe that such concepts can be assessed and taught (Pulaski, 1971; Roberts, 1976; Kirkland, 1978).

5. Integrating language arts and reading programs. Based on psycholinguistic theory, which has

102

reemphasized reading as a part of language,
efforts are being made to integrate all
learning related to reading with the child's
existing language. Therefore, today's
reading readiness programs tend to coordinate
oral language, listening, handwriting,
spelling, and reading.

6. Increased emphasis upon diagnostic-prescriptive
instruction. During the 1960's and 1970's
instruction based on children's assessed
needs--diagnostic-prescriptive instruction--
has come to the forefront. The major results
of this current emphasis on diagnostic-
prescriptive instruction are (a) recognition
that there is no single agreed-upon set of
readiness skills; (b) the development of
assessment procedures to test a variety of
skills relating to the reading readiness
program. That is, instead of assessing readiness as a unitary skill, assessment could be
made of specific subskills; and (c) the
development of a great number of programs to
teach beginning reading, each requiring a
different pattern of subskills for success.

Olson and Dillner (1982) conclude by stating that:

All these trends have resulted in changing
educators' views of reading readiness from
global to specific, so that today reading
readiness may be considered as preparation
for success in a specified reading instruction
program. Such a program will probably
implement a comprehensive approach to reading
readiness, including all the language arts
skills as well as selected cognitive skills
(such as conversation). These readiness
skills will probably be taught to all children, regardless of chronological or mental
age, and skill instruction will be based upon
a diagnosis of the specific child's needs
(p. 388).

Definitions of Reading Readiness

Bates (1977) asserts that reading readiness is a
mere slogan. She states that definitions of reading
readiness reflect the philosophical and psychological
era in which the slogan was born. She observed that
most definitions included such words as maturity,

103

stage of development and state of preparation. A
review of the literature shows that the various
definitions of reading readiness contain the components
of a slogan set down by Komisar and McClellan (1961).

1. Slogans summarize assertions -

   Reading readiness may be defined as a state
   of general maturity which, when reached,
   allows a child to learn to read without
   excess difficulty. (Harris, 1980, p. 26)

2. Slogans are more than a generalization -

   Beller (1970) states that the concept of
   readiness is too complex to lend itself to
   simplistic generalizations.

3. Slogans are descriptive of practice -

   Reading readiness, as the term implies, refers
   to the activities which schools, and homes
   provide in building the background knowledge,
   skills and attitudes which will make the
   reading process itself more effective.
   (Wagner, 1959)

4. Slogans contain a prescriptive element -

   The general stage of developmental maturity
   and preparedness at which a child can learn
   to read easily and proficiently in a regular
   classroom setting when exposed to good
   teaching. (Rogers,p. 3)

5. Slogans come to acquire an interpretation
   and summarize some definite sets of particu-
   lars -

   Perhaps the most widely accepted concept of
   readiness for reading is that it is the
   interweaving of numerous factors that permit
   a child to succeed in learning to read.
   These factors include physical, social,
   emotional, mental and language aspects of a
   child's development. (Weintraub, 1971)

6. Slogans may be systematically ambiguous -

   Although concept of reading readiness is more
   than twenty years old, its nature and purpose

104

are not universally clear to all teachers.
Readiness is a stage or period in the child's
development when he is ready to learn to read
with success and satisfaction. (Spache, 1963)

7. Slogans summarize proposals for actions -

   Reading readiness suggests that the child is
   all set to go, developed to the stage where
   he is ready to learn to read. Physically,
   intellectually, emotionally, socially--in
   every way the child's whole being is poised,
   attuned to the demands of the reading tasks,
   completely prepared for learning. (Dawson,
   1959)

Other Definitions of Reading Readiness

1. A child's readiness to read is dependent upon
   how his or her unique set of prereading
   behaviors can be matched with appropriate
   instruction (Gates, 1937; Ausubel, 1958;
   Durkin, 1976).

2. The term "readiness" for any kind of learning
   refers to the stage firstly, when the child
   can learn easily and without emotional strain,
   and secondly, when the child can learn
   profitably because efforts at teaching give
   gratifying results (Downing and Thackray,
   1975).

3. Reading readiness is defined as the stage in
   development when, either through maturation
   or through previous learning, or both, the
   individual child can learn to read easily and
   profitably (Downing and Thackray, 1975).

4. Reading readiness may be defined as a state
   of general maturity, based on aptitudes and
   learned knowledge and skills, which allows a
   child to learn to read under given instructional conditions (Harris, 1980, p. 19).

5. Another widely cited definition of readiness
   is Ausubel's statement that readiness is "the
   adequacy of existing capacity in relation to
   the demands of a given learning task" (Ausubel,
   1958). Ausubel's definition is illustrated
   in Figure I.

105

Figure I

An Illustration of Ausubel's Definition of Readiness

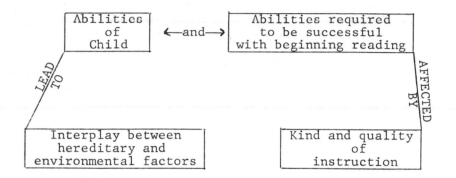

Methods for Evaluating Reading Readiness

Methods for evaluating reading readiness differ almost as widely as definitions of reading readiness. Some researchers believe that readiness can be measured by one of three methods: (1) standardized tests, (2) information obtained from the child's family, and (3) observation of the child's daily behavior (Harris and Sipay, 1980).

Standardized Tests

Intelligence tests, tests of specific abilities, and reading readiness tests are all forms of standardized tests that are used to evaluate reading readiness.

The intelligence tests used to measure reading readiness fall into two categories--group and individual.

Group Intelligence Tests. Group intelligence tests for first-grade children are all somewhat alike. Directions are given orally, and the children indicate their answers by making marks on pictures. No reading ability is involved. Items commonly included are intended to measure such abilities as range of information, understanding of single words and sentences, memory, ability to follow directions, recognition of similarities and differences, and logical reasoning.

The following group tests are recommended for use

near the end of kindergarten or beginning of the first grade:

1. The Pintner-Cunningham Primary Test, Revised 1965

2. Otis-Lennon Mental Ability Test, Primary I (Kindergarten) Primary II (First Half of Grade 1)

3. The SRA Primary Mental Abilities

4. The California Test of Mental Maturity, Pre-Primary Battery

5. The Kuhlmann-Anderson Measure of Academic Potential, Grade 1A

Individual Intelligence Tests. To obtain a measure of mental ability that is as nearly as possible a measure of the child's mental capacity, uninfluenced by emotional and social factors, it is necessary to use an individual intelligence test. The two individual intelligence tests most widely used by children in kindergarten or first grade are The revised Stanford-Binet Intelligence Scale and the Wechsler Intelligence Scale for Children-Revised (WISC-R), which provides separate verbal performance IQ's as well as a total IQ. The Wechsler Preschool and Primary Scale of Intelligence (WPPSI) is gradually replacing the WISC.

The Slosson Intelligence Test is an individual test that does not require a highly trained examiner: It has sufficient agreement with the revised Stanford-Binet and WISC to justify its use as a screening test.

Tests of Specific Abilities

1. The Illinois Test of Psycholinguistic Abilities, revised edition (ITPA), is an individual-ly administered test battery that attempts to provide a diagnostic analysis of a child's performance in receiving information (decoding), association, and expressing information (encoding); in three channels of communication (visual, auditory, and motor); and at two levels of organization (automatic-sequential or representational). It contains ten subtests and two optional subtests, providing a total score and twelve subscores.

107

2.   The Frostig Developmental Test of Visual
     Perception (DTVP) has subtests intended to
     measure five aspects of visual perception:
     eye-hand coordination, figure-ground, form
     constancy, position in space, and spatial
     relations.

3.   The Purdue Perceptual-Motor Survey is a series
     of individually administered tests of aspects
     of physical coordination and perceptual-motor
     integration, considered by Kephart to be basic
     for the development of academic achievement
     (Roach and Kephart, 1966).

Reading Readiness Tests

Traditionally, readiness tests have been administered for three purposes:

1.   To determine whether or not the child is
     indeed ready to read.

2.   To reveal--through use of the test as a
     diagnostic tool--areas of specific strengths
     and weaknesses.

3.   To determine which children to place in which
     groups for reading or for reading-readiness
     instruction. (Farr and Roser 1979, p. 108).

In selecting a readiness test, attention should be
paid to the following questions:

1.   How good is the test's validity in terms of
     predicting reading achievement? This is by
     far the most important question.

2.   Does the test have adequate reliability? For
     satisfactory measurement of individual chil-
     dren the reliability coefficient should be at
     least .90.

3.   Are the norms satisfactory? Are they based on
     a sufficiently large and representative number
     of children? Are there norms for the separate
     parts as well as for the total score?

4.   Are the directions for administering and
     scoring the test clear and complete?

5.   How time-consuming is the test to give and

score? Tests which have parts that must be given individually to each child are generally quite time-consuming. (Aukerman and Aukerman, 1981; Harris and Sipay, 1980).

6. Can a readiness test predict reading success?

7. How closely related are the purposes of this readiness test and the purposes of my instructional program?

8. Is every child ready for the readiness test?

9. Are there those who don't understand the language of the test?

10. Are there those who don't need to take a complete battery?

11. Can a readiness test help me group for reading (or readiness) instruction?

12. Can I use a readiness test as a diagnostic indicator of specific strengths and weaknesses? (Farr and Roser, 108-109).

Among the many readiness tests now available, the following are recommended:

Gates-MacGinitie Readiness Test. Beginning first grade. Listening comprehension, auditory discrimination, following directions, letter recognition, visual-motor coordination, auditory blending. A word recognition test is also included to detect early readers.

Harrison-Steoud Reading Readiness Profiles. A readiness test with five subtests: using symbols, visual discrimination, using contexts, auditory discrimination, using contexts and auditory clues; also letter names.

MacMillan Reading Readiness Tests. End of kindergarten, beginning grade 1. Subtests include a quantified rating scale, visual discrimination, auditory discrimination, vocabulary and concepts, letter names, visual motor skills.

Metropolitan Readiness Tests. 1965 Revision. Beginning grade 1. Word meaning, listening,

matching, alphabet, numbers, and copying. Forms
A, B.

Clymer-Barrett Prereading Battery. Reading readiness test that samples visual discrimination,
auditory discrimination, and visual-motor skills.
Forms A, B.

Murphy-Durrell Reading Readiness Analysis. Beginning first grade. Includes subtests on visual
discrimination, auditory discrimination (phonemes),
letter names, and learning rate.

Monroe Reading Aptitude Tests are very comprehensive, with seventeen subtests, but several parts
require individual administration and therefore
the total time required is impractical for most
schools.

The Walker Readiness Test for Disadvantaged Preschool Children is an individually administered
test taking about 10 minutes per child. It was
developed to be as culture-fair as possible and
was standardized on nearly 12,000 Head Start and
Day Care Center Children. Norms are given for
six month intervals from ages 4 to 6 years 6
months.

The Kindergarten Evaluation of Learning Potential
(KELP) consists of lessons to be used daily in
kindergarten with structured observations and a
final test providing the evaluation. Further
research is needed before a judgment can be made
about the value of such learning-testing programs
as compared with conventional readiness tests.

Research data on the effectiveness of readiness
tests to predict reading success have not been very
encouraging. Gates, Bond and Russell (1939) have
pointed out that only if the tests represent the method
of instruction to be used in teaching reading are they
useful diagnostic instruments. Comparison of readiness
tests with teachers' judgment indicate that teachers
are at least as good as readiness tests in predicting
which children will have success in beginning reading.
Kottmeyer (1947) compared teachers' ability to predict
with that of intelligence tests and readiness tests
and found that teachers' judgment were not significantly improved when the scores from intelligence and
readiness tests were added. Those teachers who had
been teaching for ten years or more were better

predictors of reading success than were less experienced
teachers. Koppman and Lapray (1969) also have reported
that teacher assessment of children's probable success
in reading is as good a predictor as is a readiness
test. Spache and Spache (1969) have stated that helping teachers judge children's competency in language
and readiness through the use of informal techniques
of assessment will increase determination of readiness.
That training of this sort is beneficial also has been
shown by Myklebust (1971) who found that classroom
teachers trained in the use of a simple checklist
instrument could successfully find children who needed
further diagnosis for possible learning disabilities.
Since previous research data on reading readiness
tests have not been encouraging, Aukerman and Aukerman
(1981) propose that

> the readiness test, the intelligence test,
> and teacher observation together provide
> the basis for an educated judgment of each
> child's relative maturity and readiness
> for formalized reading instruction. (p. 55)

Even though readiness tests have been criticized
often they can give us valuable information.

Reading-readiness tests can provide information
as to a child's relative ability to perform certain
tasks, including the ability to do the following:

1. Discriminate gross shapes and likenesses
    and/or differences.

2. Discriminate fine details and the finer
    likenesses and differences among them.

3. Identify pictures that match vocabulary
    dictated by the teacher.

4. Match word symbols that are alike.

5. Follow directions.

6. Follow from left-to-right across the page.

7. Recognize letters when dictated by teacher.

8. Recognize beginning sounds of words.

9. Discriminate endings and rhyming sounds.

111

10. Copy gestalts, letters, and/or words.

11. Select a picture that illustrates a concept or situation in a story paragraph read by the teacher.

12. Follow sequence of events in a story.

Aukerman and Aukerman (1981 p. 56.)

Teacher Judgment

Research data have already pruported that teacher judgment of reading readiness is as valid in some instances as readiness tests. What follows is a list of checklists, rating scales, etc. that can be used by teachers.

The Kindergarten Behavioral Index by Enid M. Banks, 1972.

The Prereading Rating Scale by Hall, Ribovich and Ramig, 1979.

A Childlist for the Evaluation of Readiness, Joseph Sanacare, 1973.

The Development of Reading Readiness

This section includes: (1) sources of lists of activities for developing reading readiness, (2) a list of textbook sources that include chapters on reading readiness and development, and (3) a list of commercial materials on readiness for teachers and students.

Sources of lists of activities

Bond and Wagner (1967) pp. 178-193.

Dallmann (1974) pp. 61-68, 75-77, 87-95, 136-140, 167-169, 173-174.

Ekwall (1970) pp. 71-87.

Fry (1972) p. 116.

Gallant (1970) pp. 64-74.

Harris and Smith (1972) pp. 130-175, 199-201, 251-257, 268.

112

Heilman (1968) pp. 31-52.

Herr (1970) pp. 26-34, 40-41, 51-53, 61-63, 70-73, 85-86, 100-102, 113-114, 121-122, 126-129, 149.

Spache and Spache (1973) pp. 56-64, 69-72, 74, 76-78, 82-83, 97-131.

Zintz (1970) pp. 140-143, 184, 391-396.

Materials

The Readiness Program should include more than a "Readiness Book." The following list suggests the variety of commercial material provided for prereading activities.

Peabody Language Development Kits, Levels P, I and III; L. Dunn and Jo O. Smith (Circle Pines, Minn.: American Guidance Service 1966 and Peabody Early Experience Kit (Peek, 1976)

Pre-Reading Skills Program (Chicago: Encyclopedia Brittanica Educational Corporation, 1975)

Developing Prereading Skills Kit (New York: Holt, Rinehart, 1972)

Crossties (Oklahoma City: Economy Co., 1978)

Distar Reading: Preschool (Chicago: Science Research Associates, 1971)

The Language and Thinking (Chicago: Follett, 1973)

Playway: An Interest Center Approach to Initial Education (New York: Winston Press, 1974)

Alpha Time--Reading Readiness Program (Plainview, N.Y.: New Dimensions in Education)

Listening Skills Program (Chicago: Science Research Associates, 1969)

Discoveries for Young Americans (Chicago: Rand McNally, 1976)

Language and How to Use It, Beginning Levels, (Glenview, Ill.: Scott Foresman, 1970)

Readiness Materials for the Teacher

Anderson, Paul S. 1963. Storytelling with the flannel board. Minneapolis, Minn.: T. S. Denison.

Baily, Carolyn S., and Lewis, Clara A. 1965. Favorite Stories for the Children's Hour. New York: Platt.

Henry, Mable Wright. 1967. Creative Experience in Oral Language. Urbana, Ill.: National Council of Teachers of English.

Huck, Charlotte S. 1976. Children's Literature in the Elementary School. 3rd ed. New York: Holt, Rinehart, and Winston.

McIntyre, Barbara. 1974. Creative Drama in the Elementary School. Itasca, Ill.: F. E. Peacock Publishers.

Possein, Wilma M. 1969. They All Need to Talk. New York: Appelton-Century-Crofts.

Russell, David and Russell, Elizabeth. 1959. Listening Aids Through the Grades. New York: Teachers College Press, Columbia University.

Spache, George D., and Spache, Evelyn B. 1973. Reading in the Elementary School. 3rd. Boston: Allyn and Bacon. (See pp. 119-123 and 128-129 for suggested materials to develop perceptual skills.)

Tooze, Ruth. 1959. Storytelling. New York: Prentice-Hall.

FOR USE WITH THE ELEMENTARY SCHOOL STUDENT

Developing Prereading Skills by Rachel G. Brake. New York: Holt, Rinehart, and Winston.

Directionality Program. Glendale, Calif.: Bowmar Records, INC.

Kindergarten Fun by Cole and Appleyard. Cincinnati, Ohio: McCormick-Mathers Publishing Company.

Kindergarten Readiness. New York: Harper and Row.

Learning Readiness System by Scott, Ratekin, Kramer, Nelson, and Dunbar. New York: Harper and Row.

Listening-Doing-Learning Tapes (Levels K-1) by Don Parker, and William Fryback. Chicago: Science Research Associates, Inc.

Listening Time (Albums 1-3) by Louise Bender Scott. Glendale, Calif.: Bowmar Records, Inc.

Peabody Early Experience Kit (Levels P-3) by Lloyd M. Dunn. Circle Pines, Minn.: American Guidance Service, Inc.

Peabody Language Kits (Levels P, I, II, III) by Lloyd M. Dunn et al. Circle Pines, Minn.: American Guidance Service, Inc.

Readiness for Learning Clinic by McLeod. Philadelphia: J. B. Lippincott Company.

Instructional Methods to Build Reading Readiness

Sources

At the Beginning: Reading Readiness, Chapter 3, pp. 88-144. In Roger Farr and Nancy Roser, Teaching a Child to Read. New York: Harcourt Brace Jovanovich, 1979.

Reading Readiness, Chapter 14 pp. 383-403 and Chapter 15 Teaching Word Identification, Comprehension, Study, and Readiness Skills, pp. 411-537. In JoAnne P. Olson and Martha H. Dillner, Learning to Teach Reading in the Elementary School-- Utilizing a Competency-Based Instructional System. New York: MacMillan Publishing Company, Inc., 1982.

Reading Readiness: Preparation for Reading, Chapter 7, pp. 130-163. In Susanna Whitney Pflaum, The Development of Language and Reading in the Young Child. Columbus, Ohio: Charles E. Merrill Publishing Company, 1974.

Reading Instruction, Chapter 14 (Section on Readiness for Beginning Reading, pp. 330-337). In Walter T. Petty, Dorothy C. Petty, and Marjorie F. Becking, Experience in Language Tools and Techniques for Language Arts Methods. Boston: Allyn and Bacon, Inc., 1976.

Teaching Reading Readiness Skills, Chapter 3, pp. 40-55. In JoAnne Dauzat and Sam Dauzat, Reading: The Teacher and the Learner. New York: John Wiley & Sons, 1981.

Readiness for Reading and Reading Readiness, Chapter 2, pp. 49-86. In Robert Aukerman and Louise R. Aukerman, How Do I Teach Reading? New York: John Wiley & Sons, 1981.

Readiness, Chapter 2, pp. 27-48. In J. Estill Alexander (ed.), Teaching Reading. Boston: Little, Brown and Company, 1979.

The Program and The Pupil, Chapter 1 (the section on Developing Language and Reading) pp. 27-30. In Mildred R. Donghue, The Child and the English Language Arts. Dubuque, Iowa: Wm. C. Brown Company Publishers, 1975.

Children Prepare for Reading, Chapter 3, pp. 55-94. In MaryAnne Hall, Jerilyn K. Ribovich and Christopher J. Ramig, Reading and the Elementary School Child, New York: D. Van Nostrand and Company, 1979.

Preparing to Read, Chapter 6, pp. 93-122 and Using Readiness Appraisals, Chapter 7, pp. 123-148. In Guy L. Bond and Eva Bond Wagner, Teaching the Child to Read. New York: The MacMillan Company, 1960.

The Prereading Skills, Module 3, pp. 108-165. In Charles T. Mangrum II and Harry W. Forgan. Developing Competencies in Teaching Reading--A Modular Program for Preservice and Inservice Elementary and Middle School Teachers. Columbus, Ohio: Charles E. Merrill Publishing Company, 1979.

Aids and Materials for the Readiness Program

The Montessori Circle, Square, and Triangle

Workbooks for Matching Shapes

Parquetry Blocks

Rough-Surface Letters

Mazes

Stencils

Cut Pictures

Consonant Picture Cards

Visual Perceptual Worksheets

Picture Sequence

Flannel Board

Attendance Name Cards

Object Labels

Summary of Readiness Development Section

If we as educators give our children a good start in the early years of their school career, we can alleviate many reading problems they could face in later years.

Often times, when a child begins to have problems in school, no one wants to accept responsibility. In other words, they tend to pass the buck. A poem by an unknown author describes this passing of the buck syndrome.

The college professor says:
Such rawness in a pupil is a shame,
Lack of preparation in high school is to blame.

But the high school teacher says:
Good Heavens! Such crudity; the boy's a fool.
The fault, of course, is the middle school.

But the middle school teacher says:
From such stupidity may I be spared,
They send them to me so unprepared.

But the primary teacher says:
Kindergarten blockheads, and they call
that preparation? Worse than none at all.

But the kindergarten teacher says:
Such lack of training never did I see,
What kind of mother must that mother be?

But Mother has the final word, Mother says:

117

Poor helpless child; he's not to blame,
His father's people are all the same.

But Father blurts - Don't you place upon me this blame,
I'm not even sure he's supposed to bear my name.

References and Bibliography

Arthur, G. A Quantitative Study of the Results of
Grouping First Grade Children According to Mental
Age. Journal of Educational Research, 12
(October 1925), 173-185.

Aukerman, C., and Aukerman, R. How Do I Teach Reading?
New York: John Wiley & Sons, 1981.

Ausubel, D. P. Viewpoints from Related Disciplines:
Human Growth and Development. Teachers College
Record, 60 (February 1958), 245-254.

Banks, E. M. Kindergarten Behavioral Index. Australian
Council for Educational Research, Frederick Street,
Hawthorn, Victoria 3122; 1972.

Bates, S. A. A Perspective on Slogans: Reading Readiness. An unpublished paper submitted to Ed. 272-
830 - Theory Design of Curriculum, January 12,
1977 at the University of Wisconsin-Madison.

Beller, E. K. The Concept Readiness and Several Applications. The Reading Teacher, 23 (May 1970),
727-737.

Bond, G. L. and Wagner, E. B. Teaching the child to
read. Third Edition. New York: The Macmillan
Company, 1960.

Bond, G. L. and Wagner, E. B. Teaching the child to
read. Fourth Edition. New York: The Macmillan
Company, 1966.

California Test of Mental Maturity, Pre-Primary Battery.
California Test Bureau/McGraw-Hill, Monterey, CA.

Clymer, T. and Barrett, T. C. Clymer-Barrett Prereading
Battery. Lexington, Massachusetts: Personnel
Press, 1968.

Dallmann, M., Rouch, R. L., Chang, L. Y. C., and
DeBoer, J. J. The Teaching of Reading. 4th ed.
New York: Holt, Rinehart and Winston, 1974.

Dawson, M. A., and Bammon, H. A. Fundamentals of Basic
Reading Instruction. New York: Longman, Green
& Co., Inc., 1959.

Dewey, J. The Primary Education Fetich. New York
Teachers' Monographs, (November 1896).

Downing, J., and Thackray, D. V. Reading Readiness.
London: Hodder and Stoughton for the United
Kingdom Reading Association, 1975.

Durkin, D. Reading Readiness. The Reading Teacher,
23 (March 1970), 528-34.

Durkin, D. Teaching Them to Read. Second Edition.
Boston: Allyn and Bacon, Inc., 1974.

Durkin, D. Teaching Young Children to Read. Boston:
Allyn and Bacon, 1976.

Ekwall, E. E., Locating and Correcting Reading Difficulties. Columbus, Ohio: Merrill, 1970.

Farr, R., and Roser, N. Teaching a Child to Read.
New York: Harcourt Brace Jovanovich, Inc., 1979.

Fowler, W. A. A Developmental Learning Strategy for
Early Reading in a Laboratory Nursery School.
Interchange, 2 (Winter 1971), 106-125.

Frostig Developmental Test of Visual Perception.
Publishers Test Service, Monterey, CA.

Fry, E. B. Reading Instruction for Classroom and
Clinic. New York: McGraw-Hill, 1972.

Gallant, R. Handbook in Corrective Reading: Basic
Tasks. Columbus, Ohio: Merrill, 1970.

Gates, A. The Necessary Mental Age for Beginning
Reading. Elementary School Journal, 37 (March
1937), 497-508.

Gates, A. I., Bond, G. L., and Russell, D. H. Methods
of Determining Reading Readiness. New York:
Bureau of Publications, Teachers College, Columbia
University, 1939.

Gates, A. I., and MacGinitie, W. H. Gates-MacGinitie
Readiness Skills Test. New York: Teachers
College Press.

Hall, M. A.; Ribovich, J. K. and Ramig, C. J. Reading
and the elementary school child (2nd ed.). New
York: D. Van Nostrand, 1979.
120

Harris, A. J., and Sipay, E. R. How to Increase Read-
ing Ability - A Guide to Developmental and
Remedial Methods. Seventh Edition. New York:
Longman, Inc., 1980.

Harris, L. A., and Smith, C. B. Reading Instruction
Through Diagnostic Teaching. New York: Holt,
Rinehart and Winston, 1972.

Harrison-Steoud Reading Readiness Profiles. Riverside
Publishing Co., Lombard, IL.

Heilman, A. W. Phonics in Proper Perspective. 2nd ed.
Columbus, Ohio: Merrill, 1968.

Heilman, A. W. Principles and Practices of Teaching
Reading. 3rd ed. Columbus, Ohio: Merrill, 1972.

Herr, A. E. Learning Activities for Reading. 2nd ed.
Dubuque, Iowa: Brown, 1970.

Huey, E. B. The Psychology and Pedagogy of Reading.
New York: Macmillan Publishing Co., Inc., 1908.

Illinois Test of Psycholinguistic Abilities. Western
Psychological Services, Los Angeles, CA.

Kindergarten Evaluation of Learning Potential. Webster
Division of McGraw-Hill Book Co., New York, NY.

Kirkland, E. R. A Piagetian Interpretation of Beginning Reading Instruction. The Reading Teacher,
31 (February 1978), 497-503.

Komisar, B. P., and McClellan, J. E. The Logic of
Slogans. Language and Concepts in Education.
B. Othanel Smith and Robert H. Ennis (Ed.),
Chicago: Rand McNally and Co., 1961, 195-215.

Koppman, P. S. and LaPray, M. H. Teacher Ratings and
Pupil Reading Readiness Scores. Reading Teacher,
22 (1969), 603-608.

Kottmeyer, W. Readiness for Reading, Part I and Part
II. Elementary English, 24 (1947), 355-66; 528-33.

Kuhlmann-Anderson Measure of Academic Potential.
Scholastic Testing Service, Bensenville, IL.

Lee, J. M., and Clark, W. W. Lee Clark Readiness Test.
Monterey: California Test Bureau, 1962.

MacMillan Reading Readiness Tests. MacMillan Publishing Co., Inc., New York, NY.

Metropolitan Readiness Tests. New York: Harcourt Brace Jovanovich, 1965.

Monroe Reading Aptitude Tests. Riverside Publishing Co., Lombard, IL.

Morphett, M. V., and Washburn, C. When Should Children Begin to Read? Elementary School Journal, 31 (March 1931), 496-503.

Murphy-Durrell Reading Readiness Analysis. The Psychological Corp., New York, NY.

Mykelbust, H. R. The Pupil Rating Scale: Screening for Learning Disabilities. New York: Grune and Stratton, 1971.

Olson, P. and Dillner, M. H. Learning to Teach Reading in the Elementary School--Utilizing a Competency-Based Instructional System. New York: MacMillan Publishing Co., Inc., 1976.

Olson, P. and Dillner, M. Learning to Teach Reading in the Elementary School--Utilizing a Competency-Based Instructional System. Second Edition. New York: MacMillan Publishing Co., Inc., 1982.

Otis-Lennon Mental Ability Test, Primary I and Primary II. The Psychological Corp., New York, NY.

Pflaum, S. W. The Development of Language and Reading in the Young Child. Columbus, Ohio: Charles E. Merrill Publishing Company, 1974.

Pinter-Cunningham Primary Test, Revised. Harcourt Brace Jovanovich, New York, NY.

Pulaski, M. A. Understanding Piaget. New York: Harper and Row, Publishers, 1971.

Roach, E. G., and Kephart, N. C. The Purdue Perceptual-Motor Survey. Columbus, Ohio: Charles E. Merrill, 1966.

Roberts, K. P. Piaget's Theory of Conservation and Reading Readiness. The Reading Teacher, 30 (December 1976), 246-250.

Rogers, N. What is Reading Readiness? Newark: International Reading Association. ERIC/CRIER.

Sanacare, J. A checklist for the evaluation of readiness. Elementary English, 50 (1973), 859.

Slosson Intelligence Test. Slosson Educational Publications, East Aurora, NY.

Spache, G. D., and Spache, E. B. Reading in the Elementary School. Second Edition. Boston: Allyn and Bacon, Inc., 1969.

Spache, G. D. Toward Better Reading. Champaign, Illinois: Garrard Publishing Co., 1963.

SRA Primary Mental Abilities. Science Research Associates, Inc., Chicago, IL.

Stanford-Binet Intelligence Scale - Revised. Riverside Publishing Co., Lombard, IL.

Wagner, G. W. What the Schools are Doing in Developing Reading Readiness. Education, 79, (1959), 385-387.

Walker Readiness Test for Disadvantaged Preschool Children. USOE Bureau of Research, ERIC ED 037 253.

Wechsler Intelligence Scale for Children - Revised. The Psychological Corp., New York, NY.

Wechsler Preschool and Primary Scale of Intelligence. The Psychological Corp., New York, NY.

Weintraub, S. What Research Says About Learning to Read. Coordinating Reading Instruction. Helen M. Robinson (Ed.) Chicago: Scott Foresman, 1971, 181-90.

Zintz, M. V. The Teacher and the Learner. Dubuque, Iowa: Brown, 1970.

CHAPTER FIVE

WORD IDENTIFICATION AND WORD RECOGNITION

LAWRENCE L. SMITH
UNIVERSITY OF SOUTHERN MISSISSIPPI

The trend today in reading is to emphasize comprehension. There are many educators who stress comprehension to the extent that they ignore some of the
prerequisites that are necessary for students to
comprehend the printed material. For instance, it is
generally agreed upon that one must have adequate
prior knowledge and adequate vocabulary in order to be
able to comprehend what is being read. However, it
must also be recognized that if something is being
read, one must also recognize the words in order to
be able to comprehend. In other words, the student
must recognize that c-a-t is "cat" and not "dog" or
some other word.

In order for the reader and writer to be on the
same "wave length" it is necessary to clarify the
difference between word recognition and word identification. Word identification and word recognition are
closely related features of word perception. "First
contact with a new word form calls for identification
of the printed symbol in terms of its sound and meaning. Subsequent contacts develop recognition...the
development of word recognition implies identification
as the first step in the process. Until a printed
symbol is grasped at a glance, until it has become
what we term a sight word, recognition requires some
degree of identification" (Bond, Tinker and Wasson,
1979, p. 219).

One of our goals in reading education is to teach
children to recognize words rapidly; therefore, we
must teach recognition techniques in our reading
program. We must also train students in word identification in order that the learner can develop skills
in decoding other printed forms of the words. There
are three basic word identification skills: phonics,
structural analysis and context clues. This paper
will focus predominantly on phonics and structural
analysis. It has been argued by some educators that
the teaching of phonics and structural analysis is not
necessary. They say that the English language is so
irregular that learning sound-symbol relationships is
useless. Any child who can verbalize the generalizations doesn't need phonics and structural analysis

125

instruction. It is also argued that many people can read but can't tell you the generalization or rule for various sound-symbol associations. For instance, many people could read the word c-i-t-y and pronounce the word /city/ but not be able to tell you why the c is a soft c. In other words, they would not be able to say that when c is followed by i, e, or y it usually records a soft sound of c, but yet they can read. From the first grade reading studies, sponsored by the USOE, Bond and Dykstra (1967) concluded that regardless of the approach to reading instruction used in first grade, word recognition skills must be emphasized. This was also true for second grade. One reason that we need word analysis skills is to be able to transfer sound-symbol relationships from one word to another. Sometimes when students have difficulty with comprehension, it is because they spend too much time on analysis of the words. Our task as educators is to move the student away from analyzing the words that they already know. If the child spends too much time on analysis then the passage may be too difficult and the teacher may want to give easier material for practice until the words come more easily. When the words come more easily or at an almost automatic level, then our comprehension should improve.

Powell et al. (1976) agree that many of the tasks that are done in reading are difficult for people to verbalize. However, they suggest that readers know the concept or principle and that the concept or principle operates as an unconscious response. The rules or generalizations are the surface indicators of skill identification and specification. To be a skilled reader one must know at least as much about what and why to do as one knows about how to do (Powell et al., 1976). The reading skill behaviors that Powell et al. examined in the research indicated that the skill behaviors selected tended to reflect a larger more inclusive range of behaviors that together constitute a system of concepts and principles. These concepts and principles are more powerful, more pervading, and more expansive than any one or two specific reading skill behaviors. The concepts and principles that are discussed in this paper will reflect what their research indicates are necessary concepts and principles in decoding in order to reach various levels of literacy.

The decoding concepts and principles that students should have mastered by the time they reach approximately a fourth grade reading level on a standardized

achievement test are specified in this paragraph.
First is the Speech-Sound Concept. The concept that
students must be able to use is that words are made up
of sounds and that these sounds occur in many different
words. The research on phonemic segmentations supports
this concept. The second concept is the Concept of
Order which states that there is an exact correspondence
between the order of sounds spoken and the left-to-
right sequence of words as printed. Here the student
learns to discriminate auditorially the organization
of sounds and temporal succession. They also learn
that the movement of a message is in a left-to-right
sequence. Next is the Associative Principle which
states that permanent connections can be formed between
repeated paired presentations so that presentation of
one elicits a response of the other. For example,
learning the names of the letters involves paired
associations. Also, grapheme-phoneme associations are
essential to learning to read. Names of words are
associative in nature and children must learn to call
or identify a word by its "name." Next is the
Flexibility Principle which states certain units are
equivalent so the substitution of one set of symbols
for another can be accomplished without any substantial
difference. That is, the child must learn various
orthographic styles in printed and written language.
They must learn the lower case, upper case, manuscript,
cursive as well as other print styles. The next concept is the Concept of Word Boundaries which states
that the spaces between words represent the end of one
word and the beginning of another word. While children
are learning to read they must develop an understanding
of the nature of visual units which are appropriate for
learning to read, that is, letters and words. They
need to learn that the space or blank places break the
visual components into parts. This indicates when one
word has ended and the next one begins or when a
sentence ends and the next sentence begins. Next is
the Generative Principle which states that knowledge of
elements and how to combine or blend these elements
sequentially increases the production capability of
performing significant pronunciation units. For
example, phoneme blending has a significant relationship to performance in reading. Beginning readers
need to learn to assemble and reassemble elements into
meaningful units. The Concept of a Syllable states a
vowel sound is the nucleus of the syllable and the
word has as many syllables as it has vowel sounds.
When children first learn to read, most words are
monosyllabic; however, as a child progresses in reading
more and more words are polysyllabic. A key to

127

figuring out how to pronounce difficult polysyllabic words is the power to perceive and determine the number of syllables it contains.

The major decoding concepts that students should have mastered in order to read at about a mid-fifth grade level plus or minus a half year are as follows. The Principle of Silentness states that certain letter(s) in a word are not pronounced, but are essential features in its visual structure. For instance, the phonic generalization regarding the "final e" is a discriminating skill. The next principle is the Principle of Position which states that the position of a letter(s) in a word influences the sound represented by that letter(s). Examples of the Principle of Position would be the y as a vowel and the sounds it records depending upon its position as well as other letters such as the x, the q, and the s. Next is the Principle of Variability which states the sound value of letters which represent sounds, changes from one word to another or within a word depending on adjacent letters, position, and silent letter influences. For example the letters c and g produce different sounds depending upon the letter that follows. Also the letters s, q, and x record varying sound values.

Next is the Principle of Clustering which states special sound-letter units and combinations possess particular pronunciation characteristics. An example is vowel diphthongs such as oi, oy, ou, and ow; vowel digraphs such as ai, ei, etc. and oo (the long and short sound values).

Next is the Principle of Partioning which states words can be divided into natural visual units which assist in pronunciation. For example, we have three basic syllabication rules that have been identified as necessary for the reader to use. These patterns are the vowel consonant vowel pattern, the vowel-consonant consonant-vowel and the consonant-le pattern. These patterns are very powerful and have relatively few exceptions.

The next principle is the Automaticity Principle which states words in units must be recognized in a routinely smooth and easy fashion without conscious effort or excessive duration. In other words, for a student to be able to read at about a mid-fifth grade level, most decoding functions need to be at an automatic level. One way for deciding when a student's

128

sight vocabulary is automatic is when they can complete the processing of a word while their attention moves on ahead in a text. When a student has to pay attention to the letters and their sounds or the blending of sounds into syllables, then their attention is not focused on the comprehension, but focused on word analysis. In order to read at approximately a mid-seventh grade level, the only other decoding concept that needs to be learned is the Concept of Minimal Meaning Units which states morphemic units form indivisible modifiers of meaning to the basic root. In other words, students should be proficient in the use and meanings of prefixes and suffixes as well as the root words. The affixes have been shown to make a significant contribution to increasing the level of reading comprehension. The knowledge of roots, prefixes, and suffixes is basic to word recognition and is an aid in understanding the meaning of new words.

It should be emphasized that these concepts are not the only concepts that one must be able to use in order to read proficiently; however, based on our knowledge of the research at this time these would be the concepts and principles relating to decoding that can be supported in the literature. It is not this author's intention to ignore vocabulary and comprehension; however, this paper was to focus on decoding skills and not vocabulary and comprehension. Decoding, vocabulary, and comprehension concepts are all necessary in order for one to become a proficient reader.

References

Bond, Guy L. and R. Dykstra, Coordinating Center for First Grade Reading Instruction Programs. Final Report of Project No. X-001, Contract No. OE-5-10-264. Minneapolis: University of Minnesota, 1967.

Bond, Guy L., Miles A. Tinker, Barbara B. Wasson, Reading Difficulties: Their Diagnosis and Correction (fourth edition). Englewood Cliffs, NJ: Prentice-Hall, Inc., 1979.

Powell, William R., Elroy J. Bolduc, Ruthellen Crews, Mary Kantowski, Lawrence L. Smith, Evenly Wenzel, "Project to Improve Education in the Basic Skills--Specifying Basic Skills," Technical Report No. 2. Tallahassee, FL: Department of Education, May, 1976.

CHAPTER SIX

PROJECT STUDY: AN INSTRUCTIONAL SYSTEM
FOR TEACHING STUDY SKILLS IN THE
ELEMENTARY READING PROGRAM

PATRICIA P. FRITCHIE
TROY STATE UNIVERSITY

A frequently heard comment in the classroom is
"take this word list and study it." Teachers are
continuously admonishing students whose performance is
poor with helpful advice such as, "you'll have to study
harder next time." It is generally thought that
studying occurs at the middle grades through high
school and college levels. In point of fact, formal
studying starts the first day a child enters the
school house door. However, all too infrequently,
formal instruction on how to study does not occur until
a student's high school years.

Students have been expected to learn how to study
on their own. Many students do in fact learn intu-
itively how to study and are able to design their own
workable study systems unaided. Many are not. Recently professional journals have been including articles
which extol the virtues of teaching children how to
study as part of an efficient middle grade reading
program. It is the contention of Project Study that
direct instruction in study skills should occur from
the very beginning of students' schooling.

Crawford (1973) defined study skills as the
personal means by which a student learns. These means
may include both positive and negative behaviors. It
is important that teachers help students to develop
both formal and informal study techniques that are
positive in nature.

Project Study is one way to draw attention to the
personal habits that are conducive to the development
of an efficient study system. The word Study is
turned into a five step process which will help students
to organize their study time. STUDY consists of:

S   Setting the purposes and place of study
T   Total time management
U   Undertaking a study system
D   Dividing and ordering tasks
Y   Yielding to physical and mental fatigue.

131

The first step, setting the purposes and place of the studying, helps students to become self-directing and to analyze the study problem carefully. Initially, teachers should guide students in establishing the purposes for the study sessions to insure that there is a good model for them to follow in forming goals for themselves. Setting the place to study should fit the needs of the study session. Traditionally, students have been taught that all studying should be done in a quiet area free from distractions. Current trends are to have the place of study match the goals of the learning session. If the student is to study with Mom, Dad, or someone else, then the family den or kitchen may indeed be appropriate. If individual quiet time is required for the study session then a more secluded area may be needed. The major point to be made with both students and parents is that the place to study must fit the purposes of the studying and must further be physically comfortable for the student. Dunn and Dunn (1978) listed the environmental factors that influence individual learning as: lighting, temperature, sound, and design. They contend that each individual has a preference in these environmental factors which directly affects that individual's efficiency in learning situations.

The second step involves total time management. Prior to actually beginning the study session, students should decide how long they will study, when they will begin, and the frequency of the study sessions. Students should be guided into discovering their optimum learning time and encouraged to set their study sessions within this optimum study time. Many adults have long recognized that they work better in the morning hours or that they were in fact an afternoon or evening person. While educational theory teaches that young children learn better in the morning sessions of school it is also true that children at very early ages begin to show a time preference for certain activities. For the elementary student, short periods of study at frequent intervals are usually more beneficial than one long study time. The length and the frequency of study sessions should be based on the individual child's level of maturity and intellectual ability. Students should be encouraged to make reasonable commitments for duration and frequency to honor those commitments. Gradually, as habits are formed, frequency and duration may be increased.

The third step in Project Study is to undertake a study system and to actually study. Teachers should

132

introduce the various study systems available and help students to discover the system that will work best for their study purposes and individual learning styles. In a recent study Annis and Annis (1982) found that as the grade level increased the differences in students' preferences for study techniques also increased. At the higher levels, tenth through twelfth grade, the Read only study technique lost popularity and was replaced by outlining, notetaking, reading, and combinations of all of the aforementioned techniques. Sixty percent of the students in grades six through eight who participated in this study reported that their only study technique was reading the material. Only 23% of the study's sixth through eighth grade students stated that they read and took notes. Clearly, direct instruction in the various study skills is needed.

Reading teachers have long accepted that comprehension is enhanced when the reader is actively involved with the reading process. It only stands to reason that studying would also be more efficient if the student were actively involved in the studying process. Study systems that utilize a multi-sensory approach provide this active participation.

Study systems that would be beneficial to elementary students are already the underlying organizational pattern of many educational materials. Students' attention should be directed toward this organization. One of the most commonly found study techniques is SQ3R. Developed by Robinson (1961) and based on an information processing theory of learning SQ3R works because its components are designed to help the reader deal with incoming sensory information in a more rapid and efficient manner (Tadlock, 1978).

Elementary reading teachers can help students to develop the necessary skills for using SQ3R and many other study systems by providing pre-questions for read and find out activities; as well as, having students re-read to locate specific information. Another method by which teachers aid students to gain independent study skills is to provide study guides that require the reader to actively respond to the information to be studied. These types of activities help to insure greater retention of the studied materials.

The fourth step is to divide and order the tasks to be performed. Students should learn to categorize their tasks into levels of difficulty and to divide these into the most appropriate time frame for efficient study. Again this is based on individual preference. Many students would prefer to complete the easy tasks first saving the harder ones for the bulk of study time. Other students, however, may prefer to tackle the more difficult tasks first while their minds are alert. There are no set rules. Teachers should help students to analyze their learning style to determine their preferences by conducting informal interviews.

The interview is an effective method for helping students to identify their specific learning styles. For best results the interview should be conducted in an informal and non-hurried manner. Privacy is essential if students are to engage in true intro-spection. The questions asked may include preferences for time, place, duration of study periods, intake, modality usage; as well as, attitude toward studying. It is important for the students to begin to recognize their own preferences and to establish a routine for studying. The following questions are typical of some assessment instruments and were adapted from Hill (1979):

1. How often do you read for fun?

2. How often do you read for tests?

3. When do you read mostly?

4. How do you prepare for a test?

5. What problems do you have with school assignments?

6. What is the difference between reading and studying for an assignment?

7. Do you have trouble keeping your mind on your reading?

8. Do you have trouble keeping your mind on study assignments?

9. When you have to read a chapter in your textbook how do you go about it? (Look for evidence of a systematic study system.)

10. What other study references other than textbooks do you use regularly? Occasionally?

There are also instruments on the market which would help to further identify the learning preferences of students. Dunn, Dunn, and Price (1977) designed the Learning Styles Inventory (LSI) which permits students to identify elements of their personal means of learning. Additionally, this instrument also provides a basis for teacher-student interaction. The LSI may be used with students grades three through twelve, takes approximately 30 minutes to administer, and measures environmental, emotional, sociological, and physical elements; as well as, the student's need for intake, mobility requirements, and time preferences.

The final step in Project Study is to yield to mental and physical fatigue, but not to distractions. Students should learn when to break study time to avoid frustration and overload. They should become acquainted with short tension relieving activities that would reinvigorate their minds and stimulate greater productivity. Although perserverance is a virtue its misinterpretation and the resultant unrealistic expectations may lead to a general aversion to studying altogether. Students must become aware of what their minds and bodies are saying to them and must feel the freedom to take short meaningful breaks in their study.

Using the STUDY framework, elementary teachers can direct students to form positive formal and informal study habits that will last them a lifetime. Instruction should be direct and include formal lessons on study techniques such as: SQ3R, PQRST, REAP, SQRQCQ, EVOKER, and PANORAMA. It must be pointed out that each technique serves a specific study purpose and is readily adaptable to individual needs or preferences.

SQ3R calls for the student to Survey, Question, Read, Recite, and Review. In surveying the materials to be read the student gets a mind set by looking at chapter titles, subtitles, boldface or italicized print, introductory and summary paragraphs. The reader also examines graphic aids. The survey step provides the reader with an overview of the reading assignment.

The second step calls for the reader to form questions about the reading selection and the information to be learned from the selection. Students may form questions about what they need or want to find out thereby establishing the purposes for reading.

135

Authors will often provide study questions with the
reading selection. Students should be encouraged to
read these prior to reading the selection and to add
these questions to those that they have formed themselves. Doing this provides direction to the reading
assignment and serves as an aid to comprehension. If
questions do not appear in the students' text, teachers
may choose to give a handout with some study questions
that the readers will answer. This will help students
to learn how to begin to form meaningful questions.
Additionally, students should be encouraged to turn
titles, subtitles, and boldface print into questions
to be answered during the reading.

The next step in SQ3R is to read the material. As
previously mentioned, when students are actively
involved with reading comprehension is enhanced. An
effective way of insuring active reading is to have
students look for the answers to the questions they
have formulated or that the author and/or teacher
have provided.

The fourth step may be formal or informal as it
requires the recitation of the located answers to
questions. Students may recite to themselves the
answers as they find them or they may write them forming a study guide for later usage. Writing the
answers gives the student a record for the last step
which is to review.

During the review step students re-read portions
of the selection or notes that were taken during the
reading. Again the decision whether to use an informal
approach or the more formal steps in this step is up to
individual preferences and needs.

The PQRST system developed for use by the Air
Force in training officers is very similar to SQ3R.
The student begins by previewing the reading selection.
As before attention is paid to titles, subtitles,
boldface or italicized print. Then the student forms
questions about the reading material by turning the
titles, etc. into things to read and find out about.
The third step in this system is to read the selection
and to summarize what has been read. The summary step
may be formal, written, or informal. The last is to
test to see how much information has been retained.
The student makes up the test from the questions that
have been formulated in step two of the system. Other
questions that were formed during the reading or those
provided by the author and/or teacher may also be used

in the testing stage. It is important to point out
that this testing is conducted by the student and is
evaluated by the student as a self-directed effort.
These test results should not be graded as this may
inhibit the student's willingness to use the techniques as a study aid. The testing step allows
students to determine for themselves where they need
to redirect their study efforts. It also provides
immediate feedback and self-evaluation which can lead
to the development of an independent self-reliant
student with good organizational skills.

SQ3R and PQRST are commonly used with the content
studies, but are adaptable to many situations. SQRQCQ
was designed by Fay (1965) to meet the study needs of
the mathematics student. The steps are similar to the
previously mentioned techniques but vary slightly as
the subject requires. In SQRQCQ the steps are: survey
to get a general idea of the problem's nature; question
to determine what is being asked in the problem; read
carefully looking for the details and/or relationships;
question to determine which matehmatical operations
may be needed to solve the problem and in what order
the operations should be performed; compute or solve
to find the answer; and finally question by checking
the entire process evaluating to see if the correct
solution has been reached.

A study system that lends itself well to reading
prose, poetry, and drama was developed by Pauk (1963).
EVOKER calls for the student to explore by reading the
entire selection silently to interpret mood, feelings,
and/or intent of the author's meaning. Secondly, the
student makes notes of the vocabulary, looks up key
words and/or unfamiliar words and names. Next, the
reader reads the passage orally with expression and
interprets the mood of the piece. In the fourth step
the key ideas are located and the organization of the
selection is explored. Then the student evaluates the
words, the plot, and the organization to determine how
effectively the author has developed the main ideas.
The last step is to re-read the entire selection.
Students of all ages and academic levels can be helped
to read critically by using this system.

A more recently developed technique to use with
prose is the REAP technique (Eanet and Manzo, 1976).
This system provides teachers with a method for guiding
students through an interaction with an author's ideas.
Fully developed as an independent technique, it provides
a vehicle for involving students with a direct,

137

purposeful interaction with the text. The first step
is to read the selection. Students then encode the
author's meaning into their own words. The third step,
annotating, calls for the students to write their
interpretation of the author's ideas for sharing with
others. Lastly, the student ponders the importance of
the annotation.

PANORAMA is an eight step procedure which is
sub-divided into three stages. The first stage consists of: the preparatory step in which the student
establishes the purposes for reading the passage; then
the student adapts the rate of reading to fit the
purposes of the reading selection; next the student
establishes the need to pose questions. If there is
a need the student forms those questions prior to
moving to the second stage of the procedure, the
intermediate stage.

The intermediate stage calls for an overview of
the reading selection. This step is similar to the
survey steps in SQ3R and PQRST. Next, the reader reads
and relates past knowledge to the new information. The
final step in the intermediate stage is to annotate.
Students in this step make notes on the ideas expressed
by the author or on the important information revealed
in the reading selection.

The conclusion stage is optional and may be left
out altogether. In this stage the student memorizes
information contained in the notes, outlines, and
summaries that have been made on the reading selection.
The last step in the PANORAMA system is for the students to assess their own efforts toward achievement
of their established purposes for reading; as well as,
how much of the information they have been able to
retain. The assess step may take the form of the test
step in PQRST, or may be less formal depending on
individual need and preference.

Having good study habits coupled with an efficient
study system does not insure immediate academic success
for all students. Many poor readers suffer in study-
reading assignments because they have inadequate
abilities to integrate and assimilate the materials
read (Dechant, 1982). Specifically, poor readers may
lack abilities in functional reading skills.

All reading teachers from the lowest through the
highest levels should know what the functional reading
skills are and should provide direct instruction in

these. There are various lists of these skills.
Basically, all the lists contain the following major
areas: locational skills as evidenced by usage of
indices, table of contents, and heading; reference
skills which include using dictionaries, encyclopedias,
periodicals, and other resource materials; interpretation of graphics; the adjustment of reading rate to fit
the purposes and nature of the reading selection; and
the ability to organize and restructure the information
that is taken in through outlining, and notetaking
(Harris and Sipay, 1980).

The reading teacher's role in the development of
a student's study skills requires careful diagnosis of
a student's skills in functional reading; as well as,
direct purposeful instruction in functional reading
skills. One of the least taught of these functional
reading skills is that of notetaking.

Elementary students, grades three and up, may
profit from learning a variation of the notetaking
system developed by Palmatier (1973). The student
folds a sheet of 8½" x 11" paper into thirds. This is
sometimes best done across the length or sideways with
the younger child. A line is drawn down each fold
line so that the paper now contains three equal
columns. The first column is used when previewing the
reading selection and is labeled Questions to be
answered. Here the student will write the questions
that are formed from the titles, subtitles, and/or
boldface print. Students should be cautioned to leave
ample room between the questions. Experience has
taught that a maximum of three questions per page
should be permitted. The second column labeled, What
the textbook has to say about the question, is used as
the student reads the selection. As answers to the
questions in column one are found they are written in
the student's own words. The third column is reserved
for class notes and/or information gathered from other
sources.

These notes can then be used as an effective means
of studying by simply folding column three over column
two. Now only column one should be visible and the
student may then proceed to self-test to determine what
needs to be studied more and/or reread. The student
may read the questions and recite the answers aloud,
checking each answer or just prior to a test the
student may wish to write the answers to all the questions and then check to see how much is known.

139

Educators have recognized the need for building good study habits. The true key to successful development of efficient study skills is not whether or not the student can tell you how to study effectively, but whether or not the student personally adopts a system and then personalizes that system to fit learning needs. The teacher's role is to help individuals learn, through direct instruction, the various systems that are available and to become aware of their own learning styles and needs.

In summary, Project Study is an attempt to help the classroom teacher organize the many varied aspects of developing self-reliant efficient students who possess solid study skills. There is no system that would or should substitute for direct instruction by a competent and caring classroom teacher. The one best method for teaching or instilling study skills is to begin the lessons early in a student's school career and to follow through with these teachings as systematically as we do with other curricular areas.

References

Annis, L. F. & Annis, D. B. "A normative study of student's reported preferred study techniques." Reading World, 1982, 21, 201-207.

Crawford, M. Teaching study skills. Dansville, N.Y.: Instructor Pub. 1973.

Dechant, E. V. Improving the teaching of reading (3rd Ed.) Englewood Cliffs, New Jersey: Prentice Hall. 1982.

Dunn, R. & Dunn, K. Teaching students through their individual learning styles: A practical approach. Reston, VA: Reston Pub. Co., Inc. 1978.

Dunn, R., Dunn, K. and Price, G. "Learning as a matter of style." The Journal, New York: School Administrators' Association of New York, 6, 11-12.

Eanet, M. C. & Manzo, A. V. "REAP: A strategy for improving reading/writing and study skills." Journal of Reading, 1976, 19, 647-652.

Fay, L. "Reading study skills: Math and science," Reading and Inquiry. J. A. Figurel ed., Newark, Del.: International Reading Association, 1965.

Harris, A. J. & Sipay, E. R. How to increase reading ability (7th Ed.) New York: Longman. 1980.

Hill, W. R. Secondary school reading: Process, program, procedure. Boston: Allyn and Bacon, Inc. 1979.

Palmatier, R. A. "A notetaking system for learning." Journal of Reading, 1973, 17, 36-39.

Pauk, W. "On scholarship: Advise to high school students." The Reading Teacher, 1963, 17, 73-78.

Robinson, F. P. Effective Study, (revised ed.) New York: Harper and Row, 1961.

Tadlock, D. F. "SQ3R why it works, based on an information process theory of learning." Journal of Reading, 1978, 22, 110-112.

Abelson, R. P. 39
Adams, M. J. 39, 40, 60
Adams, M. L. 1, 8, 9
Alexander, J. E. 116
Anderson   121
Anderson, P. S. 114
Anderson, R. C. 30, 40, 58, 60, 66
Anderson, R. I. 60
Anderson, T. H. 28, 29, 44, 55, 60
Andrew, M. D. 1, 9
Annis, D. B. 132, 140
Annis, L. F. 132, 140
Appleyard   114
Armbruster, B. B. 28, 29, 60
Arthur, G. 101, 119
Aukermann, C. 109, 111, 112, 116, 119
Aukermann, L. R. 109, 111, 112, 116, 119
Austin, M. C. 1, 8, 9
Ausubel, D. P. 105, 106, 119

Bader, L. A. 91, 97
Baily, C. S. 114
Baker, L. 39, 60
Ball, S. 69, 94
Ballochey, E. L. 72, 97
Bammon, H. A. 119
Banks, E. M. 112, 119
Barrett, T. C. 119
Bates, S. A. 103,119
Becking, M. F. 115
Beller, E. K. 104, 119
Binet   123
Bolduc, E. J. 129
Bond, G. L. 110, 112, 116, 119, 120, 124, 125, 129
Bormuth, J. R. 26, 60
Brake, R. G. 114
Bransford, J. D. 56, 61
Brooker, I. A. 25
Browder, R. 83, 94
Brown, A. L. 39, 60, 61
Brown, H. A. 23, 47, 61
Bruce, B. 60
Bruno, J. E. 47, 62
Buckner, J. 88, 98
Burke, C. L. 23, 63
Buros, O. K. 25, 61
Butkowsky, I. S. 73, 94

Callis, R. 63

143

147

Mothner, H. 84, 98
Muller, D. 71, 95
Muller, K. E. 60
Murphy   122
Myklebust, H. R. 111, 122

Nelson   115
Neufeld, J. S. 71, 98
Nicholas, D. N. 37, 68
Northcutt, N. 28, 65

Olivarez   47
Olson, J. P. 102, 103, 115, 122
O'Neil, E. 87
Ortony, A. 39, 40, 66
Osgood, C. E. 76, 98
Otis   122
Otto, W. 8, 9

Page, W. D. 80, 98
Palmatier, R. A. 138, 140
Pankratz, R. 1, 9
Parker, D. 115
Pauk, W. 136, 140
Pavlik, R. A. 2, 9
Pearson, P. D. 39, 65
Petty, D. C. 115
Petty, W. T. 115
Pflaum, S. W. 115, 122
Pinnell, G. S. 80, 98
Pinter   122
Pintner, R. 23, 66
Possein, W. M. 114
Powell, W. R. 125, 129
Powers, S. 47, 66
Prendergast, J. 89, 95
Price, G. 134, 140
Pulaski, M. A. 102, 122

Rabban, E. 92, 98
Ramig, C. J. 112, 116, 120
Ramsey, I. L. 85, 98
Ratekin   115
Rayner, K. 30, 65
Redish, J. C. 28, 63, 66
Reilly, T. F. 71, 99
Reynolds, R. E. 30, 66
Ribovich, J. K. 112, 116, 120
Richards, H. C. 76, 95
Richek, M. A. 39, 66
Rivera, C. 66

Rivers, S. N. 85, 98
Roach, E. G. 108, 122
Roberts, K. P. 102, 122
Robinson, F. P. 132, 140
Rodick, J. D. 86, 98
Rodriguez   47
Rogers, N. 104, 123
Rosenberg, M. 70, 98
Roser, N. 108, 109, 115, 120
Rouch, R. L. 119
Royer, J. M. 25, 40, 41, 42, 47, 55, 66
Rumelhart, D. E. 39, 40, 66
Russell, D. H. 110, 114
Russell, E. 114, 120
Rust, L. W. 72, 98

Sachs, J. S. 40, 67
Sahers, D. 47, 66
Sanacare, J. 112, 123
Schank, R. C. 39, 67
Schillereff, T. A. 85, 96
Schlessinger, I. M. 26, 67
Schrank, F. A. 90, 98
Schubert, D. G. 92, 93, 99
Schubert, W. H. 73, 95
Schuman, R. B. 78, 99
Scott, L. B. 115
Searle, J. R. 39, 67
Shank, S. 25
Sharp, W. 83, 99
Shawn, K. 82, 99
Shoemaker, A. L. 71, 99
Sipay, E. R. 73, 74, 77, 96, 106, 109, 121, 138, 140
Slosson   123
Smith, C. B. 112, 121
Smith, D. L. 90, 97
Smith. L. L. 12, 13, 14, 17, 124, 129
Smith, P. L. 54, 63
Smith, R. J. 8, 9
Spache, E. B. 111, 113, 114, 123
Spache, G. D. 105, 111, 113, 114, 123
Spiro, R. J. 30, 67
Steffenson, M. S. 30, 67
Stein, N. L. 39, 67
Steoud   121
Sticht, T. G. 28, 67, 68
Strang, R. 58, 68
Streby, W. J. 64
Strelecki, K. 83, 99
Suci, G. J. 76, 98
Surber, J. R. 54, 63

Swanson, D. M. 81, 95

Tadlock, D. F. 132, 140
Tannenbaum, P. H. 76, 98
Thackray, D. V. 105, 120
Thorndike, E. L. 86, 99
Thorndyke, P. W. 39, 68
Tinker, M. A. 124, 129
Tone, B. 21
Tooze, R. 114
Torrence, E. P. 72, 99
Trabasso, T. 37, 40, 68
Traxler   25
Tuinman, J. J. 25, 41, 68

Vancil, M. 90, 99
van Dijk, T. A. 39, 64, 68
Vawter, J. M. 90, 99
Vidler, D. 78, 99

Wagner, G. W. 104, 112, 116, 119, 123
Walker   123
Walker, J. A. 91, 97
Wardrop, J. L. 55, 60, 65
Warren, W. H. 37, 68
Washburn, C. 101, 122
Wasson, B. B. 124, 129
Watson, J. 78
Wechsler   123
Weintraub, S. 104, 123
Weiser, Z. 26, 67
Wenzel, E. 129
Whaley, W. J. 71, 99
Wheeler, L. 71, 99
Wilson, S. J. 30, 65
Winograd, P. 30, 61
Willows, D. M. 73, 94
Wlodkowski, R. 75, 100
Wooden, S. 71, 95
Woodward, V. A. 23, 63
Wright, G. 85, 100

Yarborough, B. H. 72, 100
Yerkes   72

Zeno, S. 41, 55, 64
Zibart, R. 84, 100
Zintz, M. V. 113, 123

Dr. Roger J. De Santi is an Associate Professor of Reading and Coordinator of Graduate Program in the Department of Curriculum and Instruction, College of Education, University of New Orleans. He earned a B.A. in English from St. Francis College, a M.Ed. in Special Education from Boston University, and a Ed.D. in Reading from Indiana University. His teaching experiences have included the Eden-Baychester Learning Clinic, the Horace Mann School for the Deaf, the Boston University Speech and Hearing Center, and the Indiana University Institute for Child Study.

He is presently editor of the Reading: Exploration and Discovery journal and has fulfilled editorial responsibilities for numerous journals and the college divisions of several publishing houses. He has written many publications and is the author of Trends and Issues of Diagnostic and Remedial Reading also published by the University Press of America.